I0161858

The Renegade by Philip Massinger

Aka The Renegado

Philip Massinger was baptized at St. Thomas's in Salisbury on November 24th, 1583.

Massinger is described in his matriculation entry at St. Alban Hall, Oxford (1602), as the son of a gentleman. His father, who had also been educated there, was a member of parliament, and attached to the household of Henry Herbert, 2nd Earl of Pembroke. The Earl was later seen as a potential patron for Massinger.

He left Oxford in 1606 without a degree. His father had died in 1603, and accounts suggest that Massinger was left with no financial support this, together with rumours that he had converted to Catholicism, meant the next stage of his career needed to provide an income.

Massinger went to London to make his living as a dramatist, but he is only recorded as author some fifteen years later, when The Virgin Martyr (1621) is given as the work of Massinger and Thomas Dekker.

During those early years as a playwright he wrote for the Elizabethan stage entrepreneur, Philip Henslowe. It was a difficult existence. Poverty was always close and there was constant pleading for advance payments on forthcoming works merely to survive.

After Henslowe died in 1616 Massinger and John Fletcher began to write primarily for the King's Men and Massinger would write regularly for them until his death.

The tone of the dedications in later plays suggests evidence of his continued poverty. In the preface of The Maid of Honour (1632) he wrote, addressing Sir Francis Foljambe and Sir Thomas Bland: "I had not to this time subsisted, but that I was supported by your frequent courtesies and favours."

The prologue to The Guardian (1633) refers to two unsuccessful plays and two years of silence, when the author feared he had lost popular favour although, from the little evidence that survives, it also seems he had involved some of his plays with political characters which would have cast shadows upon England's alliances.

Philip Massinger died suddenly at his house near the Globe Theatre on March 17th, 1640. He was buried the next day in the churchyard of St. Saviour's, Southwark, on March 18th, 1640. In the entry in the parish register he is described as a "stranger," which, however, implies nothing more than that he belonged to another parish.

Index of Contents

THE RENEGADE aka The Renegado

DRAMATIS PERSONSAE
Asambeg, Viceroy of Tunis
Mustapha, Basha of Aleppo
Vitelli, a Venetian gentleman, disguised as a merchant
Francisco, a Jesuit
Antonio Grimaldi, the RENEGADO
Carazie, a Eunuch
Gazet, Servant to Vitelli
Aga.
Capiaga.
Janizaries.
Master.

Boatswain.
Sailors
A Gaoler. Turks
Donusa, Niece to Amurath
Paulina, Sister to Vitelli
Manto, Servant to Donusa,

SCENE: Tunis.

ACT I.

SCENE I. A Street Near the Bazaar

Enter **VITELLI** and **GAZET**.

VITELLI
You have hired a shop, then?

GAZET
Yes, sir; and our wares,
Though brittle as a maidenhead at sixteen,
Are safe unladen; not a crystal crack'd,
Or China dish needs soldering; our choice pictures,
As they came from the workman, without blemish:
And I have studied speeches for each piece,
And, in a thrifty tone, to sell them off,
Will swear by Mahomet and Termagant,
That this is mistress to the great duke of
Florence,
That, niece to old king Pepin, and a third,
An Austrian princess by her Roman nose,
Howe'er my conscience tells me they are figures
Of bawds and common courtezans in Venice.

VITELLI
You make no scruple of an oath, then?

GAZET
Fie, sir!
'Tis out of my indentures; I am bound there,
To swear for my master's profit, as securely
As your intelligencer must for his prince,
That sends him forth an honourable spy,
To serve his purposes. And, if it be lawful

In a Christian shopkeeper to cheat his father,
I cannot find but to abuse a Turk
In the sale of our commodities, must be thought
A meritorious work.

VITELLI
I wonder, sirrah,
What's your religion?

GAZET
Troth, to answer truly,
I would not be of one that should command me
To feed upon poor John, when I see pheasants
And partridges on the table: nor do I like
The other, that allows us to eat flesh
In Lent, though it be rotten, rather than be
Thought superstitious; as your zealous cobler,
And learned botcher, preach at Amsterdam,
Over a hotchpotch. I would not be confined
In my belief: when all your sects and sectaries
Are grown of one opinion, if I like it,
I will profess myself, in the mean time,
Live I in England, Spain, France, Rome,
Geneva,
I'm of that country's faith.

VITELLI
And what in Tunis?
Will you turn Turk here?

GAZET
No: so I should lose
A collop of that part my Doll enjoin'd me
To bring home as she left it: 'tis her venture,
Nor dare I barter that commodity,
Without her special warrant.

VITELLI
You are a knave, sir:
Leaving your roguery, think upon my business,
It is no time to fool now.
Remember where you are too: though this mart time
We are allow'd free trading, and with safety,
Temper your tongue, and meddle not with the Turks,
Their manners, nor religion.
Gas. Take you heed, sir,
What colours you wear. Not two hours since, there landed
An English pirate's whore, with a green apron,

And, as she walked the streets, one of their muftis,
We call them priests at Venice, with a razor
Cuts it off, petticoat, smock and all, and leaves her
As naked as my nail; the young fry wondering
What strange beast it should be. I scaped a scouring
My mistress's busk point, of that forbidden colour,
Then tied my codpiece; had I been discover'd,
I had been capon'd.

VITELLI
And had been well served.
Haste to the shop, and set my wares in order,
I will not long be absent.

GAZET
Though I strive, sir,
To put off melancholy, to which you are ever
Too much inclined, it shall not hinder me,
With my best care to serve you.

[Exit.

[Enter **FRANCISCO**.

VITELLI
I believe thee.
O welcome, sir! stay of my steps in this life,
And guide to all my blessed hopes hereafter.
What comforts, sir? Have your endeavours prosper'd?
Have we tired Fortune's malice with our sufferings?
Is she at length, after so many frowns,
Pleased to vouchsafe one chee'rful look upon us?

FRANCISCO
You give too much to fortune and your passions,
O'er which a wise man, if religious, triumphs.
That name fools worship; and those tyrants, which
We arm against our better part, our reason,
May add, but never take from our afflictions.

VITELLI
Sir, as I am a sinful man, I cannot
But like one suffer.

FRANCISCO
I exact not from you
A fortitude insensible of calamity,
To which the saints themselves have bow'd and shown

They are made of flesh and blood; all that I challenge,
Is manly patience. Will you, that were train'd up
In a religious school, where divine maxims
Scorning comparison with moral precepts,
Were daily taught you, bear your constancy's trial,

Not like Vitelli, but a village nurse,
With curses in your mouth, tears in your eyes?
How poorly it shows in you.

VITELLI
I am school'd, sir,
And will hereafter, to my utmost strength,
Study to be myself.

FRANCISCO
So shall you find me
Most ready to assist you; neither have I
Slept in your great occasions: since I left you,
I have been at the viceroy's court, and press'd,
As far as they allow, a Christian entrance;
And something I have learn'd, that may concern
The purpose of this journey.

VITELLI
Dear sir, what is 'it?

FRANCISCO
By the command of Asambeg, the viceroy,
The city swells with barbarous pomp and pride,
For the entertainment of stout Mustapha,
The basha of Aleppo, who in person
Comes to receive the niece of Amurath,
The fair Donusa, for his bride.

VITELLI
I find not
How this may profit us.

FRANCISCO
Pray you, give me leave.
Among the rest that wait upon the viceroy,
Such as have, under him, command in Tunis,
Who, as you've often heard, are all false pirates,
I saw the shame of Venice, and the scorn
Of all good men, the perjured RENEGADE;
Antonio Grimaldi.

VITELLI

Ha! his name
Is poison to me.

FRANCISCO

Yet again?

VITELLI

I have done, sir.

FRANCISCO

This debauch'd villain, whom we ever thought
(After his impious scorn done, in St. Mark's,
To me, as I stood at the holy altar)
The thief that ravish'd your fair sister from, you,
The virtuous Paulina, not long since,
As I am truly given to understand,
Sold to the viceroy a fair Christian virgin
On whom, maugre his fierce and cruel nature,
Asambeg dotes extremely.

VITELLI

'Tis my sister:
It must be she, my better angel tells me
'Tis poor Paulina. Farewell all disguises!
I'll show, in my revenge, that I am noble.

FRANCISCO

You are not mad?

VITELLI

No, sir; my virtuous anger
Makes every vein an artery; I feel in me
The strength of twenty men; and, being arm'd
With my good cause, to wreak wrong'd innocence,
I dare alone run to the viceroy's court,
And with this poniard, before his face,
Dig out Grimaldi's heart.

FRANCISCO

Is this religious?

VITELLI

Would you have me tame now?
Can I know my sister
Mew'd up in his seraglio, and in danger
Not alone to lose her honour, but her soul;
The hell-bred villain by too, that has sold both

To black destruction, and not haste to send him
To the devil, his tutor? To be patient now,
Were, in another name, to play the pander
To the viceroy's loose embraces, and cry aim!
While he, by force or flattery, compels her
To yield her fair name up to his foul lust,
And, after, turn apostata to the faith
That she was bred in.

FRANCISCO
Do but give me hearing,
And you shall soon grant how ridiculous
This childish fury is. A wise man never
Attempts impossibilities; 'tis as easy
For any single arm to quell an army,
As to effect your wishes. We come hither
To learn Paulina's fate, and to redeem her:
Leave your revenge to heaven. I oft have told you
Of a relic that I gave her, which has power,
If we may credit holy men's traditions,
To keep the owner free from violence:
This on her breast she wears, and does preserve
The virtue of it, by her daily prayers.
So, if she fall not by her own consent,
Which it were sin to think, I fear no force.
Be, therefore, patient; keep this borrow'd shape,
Till time and opportunity present us
With some fit means to see her; which perform'd,
I'll join with you in any desperate course
For her delivery.

VITELLI
You have charm'd me, sir,
And I obey in all things: pray you, pardon
The weakness of my passion.

FRANCISCO
And excuse it.
Be cheerful, man; for know that good intents
Are, in the end, crown'd with as fair events.

[Exeunt.

SCENE II. A Room in Donusa's Palace

Enter **DONUSA, MANTO**, and **CARAZIE**.

DONUSA

Have you seen the Christian captive,
The great basha is so enamour'd of?

MANTO

Yes, and it please your excellency,
I took a full view of her, when she was
Presented to him.

DONUSA

And is she such a wonder,
As 'tis reported?

MANTO

She was drown'd in tears then,
Which took much from her beauty; yet, ire spite
Of sorrow, she appear 'd the mistress of
Most rare perfections; and, though low or stature,
Her well-proportion'd limbs invite affection
And, when she speaks, each syllable is music
That does enchant the hearers: but your highness,
That are not to be parallel'd, I yet never-
Beheld her equal.

DONUSA

Come, you flatter me;
But I forgive it. We, that are born great.
Seldom distaste our servants, though they give us
More than we can pretend to. I have heard
That Christian ladies live with much more freedom
Than such as are born here. Our jealous
Turks,
Never permit their fair wives to be seen,
But at the public bagnios, or the mosques,
And, even then, veil'd and guarded. Thou,
Carazie,
Wert born in England; what's the custom: there,
Among your women? Come, be free and merry:
I am no severe mistress; nor hast thou met with
A heavy bondage.

CARAZIE

Heavy! I was made lighter
By two stone weight, at least, to be fit to serve you.
But to your question, madam; women in England,
For the most part, live like queens. Your country ladies
Have liberty to hawk, to hunt, to feast,

To give free entertainment to all comers,
To talk, to kiss; there's no such thing known there
As an Italian girdle. Your city dame,
Without leave, wears the breeches, has her husband
At as much command as her 'prentice; and, if need be,
Can make him cuckold by her father's copy.

DONUSA
But your court lady?

CARAZIE
She, I assure you, madam,
Knows nothing but her will; must be allow'd
Her footmen, her caroch, her ushers, pages,
Her doctor, chaplains; and, as I have heard,
They're grown of late so learn'd, that they maintain
A strange position, which their lords, with all
Their wit, cannot confute.

DONUSA
What's that, I prithee?

CARAZIE
Marry, that it is not only fit, but lawful,
Your madam there, her much rest and high feeding
Duly consider'd, should, to ease her husband,
Be allow'd a private friend: they have drawn a bill
To this good purpose, and, the next assembly,
Doubt not to pass it.

DONUSA
We enjoy no more,
That are o' the Othoman race, though our religion
Allows all pleasure. I am dull: some music.
Take my chapines off. So, a lusty strain.

[A **GALLIARD**. Knocking within.

Who knocks there?

[**MANTO** goes to the door, and returns.

MANTO
'Tis the basha of Aleppo,
Who humbly makes request he may present
His service to you.

DONUSA

Reach a chair. We must
Receive him like ourself, and not depart with
One piece of ceremony, state, and greatness,
That may beget respect and reverence
In one that's born our vassal. Now admit him.

[Enter **MUSTAPHA**; he puts off his yellow pantofles.

MUSTAPHA
The place is sacred; and I am to enter
The room where she abides, with such devotion
As pilgrims pay at Mecca, when they visit
The tomb of our great prophet.

[Kneels.

DONUSA
Rise; the sign

[**CARAZIE** takes up the pantofles.

That we vouchsafe your presence.

MUSTAPHA
May those Powers
That raised the Othoman empire, and still guard it,
Reward your highness for this gracious favour
You throw upon your servant! It hath pleased
The most invincible, mightiest Amurath,
(To speak his other titles would take from him
That in himself does comprehend all greatness,)
To make me the unworthy instrument
Of his command. Receive, divinest lady,

[Delivers a letter.

This letter, sign'd by his victorious hand,
And made authentic by the imperial seal.
There, when you find me mention'd, far be it from you
To think it my ambition to presume
At such a happiness, which his powerful will,
From his great mind's magnificence, not my merit,
Hath shower'd upon me. But, if your consent
Join with his good opinion and allowance,
To perfect what his favours have begun,
I shall, in my obsequiousness and duty,
Endeavour to prevent all just complaints,
Which want of will to serve you may call on me.

DONUSA

His sacred majesty writes here, that your valour
Against the Persian hath so won upon him,
That there's no grace or honour in his gift,
Of which he can imagine you unworthy;
And, what's the greatest you can hope, or aim at,
It is his pleasure you should be received
Into his royal family provided,
For so far I am unconfined, that I
Affect and like your person. I expect not
The ceremony which he uses in
Bestowing of his daughters and his nieces:
As that he should present you for my slave,
To love you, if you pleased me; or deliver
A poniard, on my least dislike, to kill you.
Such tyranny and pride agree not with
My softer disposition. Let it suffice,
For my first answer, that thus far I grace you:

[Gives him her hand to kiss.

Hereafter, some time spent to make enquiry
Of the good parts and faculties of your mind,
You shall hear further from me.

MUSTAPHA

Though all torments
Really suffer'd, or in hell imagined
By curious fiction, in one hour's delay
Are wholly comprehended; I confess
That I stand bound in duty, not to check at
Whatever you command, or please to impose,
For trial of my patience.

DONUSA

Let us find
Some other subject; too much of one theme cloys me:
Is 't a full mart?

MUSTAPHA

A confluence of all nations
Are met together: there's variety, too,
Of all that merchants traffic for.

DONUSA

I know not
I feel a virgin's longing to descend

So far from my own greatness, as to be.
Though not a buyer, yet a looker on
Their strange commodities.

MUSTAPHA
 If without a train
You dare be seen abroad, I'll dismiss mine,
And wait upon you as a common man,
And satisfy your wishes.

DONUSA
I embrace it.
Provide my veil; and, at the postern gate,
Convey us out unseen. I trouble you.

MUSTAPHA
It is my happiness you deign to
command me.

[Exeunt.

SCENE III. The Bazar

GAZET in his Shop; **FRANCISCO** and **VITELLI** walking before it.

GAZET
What do you lack? Your choice
China dishes, your pure Venetian crystal of
all sorts, of all neat and new fashions, from
the mirror of the madam, to the private
utensil of her chambermaid; and curious
pictures of the rarest beauties of Europe:
What do you lack, gentlemen?

FRANCISCO
Take heed, I say; howe'er it mayappear
Impertinent, I must express my love,
My advice, and counsel. You are young, Vitelli,
And may be tempted; and these Turkish dames,
(Like English mastiffs, that increase their fierceness
By being chain'd up,) from the restraint of freedom,
If lust once fire their blood from a fair object,
Will run a course the fiends themselves would shake at,
To enjoy their wanton ends.

VITELLI

Sir, you mistake me:
I am too full of woe, to entertain
One thought of pleasure, though all Europe's queens
Kneel'd at my feet, and courted me; much less
To mix with such, whose difference of faith
Must, of necessity, (or I must grant
Myself neglectful of all you have taught me,)
Strangle such base desires.

FRANCISCO
Be constant in
That resolution; I'll abroad again,
And learn, as far as it is possible,
What may concern Paulina. Some two hours
Shall bring me back.

[Exit.

VITELLI
All blessings wait upon you!

GAZET
Cold doings, sir? a mart do you call this? 'slight!
A pudding-wife, or a witch with a thrum cap,
That sells ale underground to such as come
To know their fortunes in a dead vacation,
Have, ten to one, more stirring.

VITELLI
We must be patient.

GAZET
Your seller by retail ought to be angry,
But when he's fingering money.

[Enter **GRIMALDI, MASTER, BOATSWAIN, SAILORS,** and **TURKS**.

VITELLI
Here are company

Defend me, my good angel,

[Seeing **GRIMALDI**.

I behold
A basilisk!

GAZET

What do you lack? what do you lack? pure China dishes, clear crystal glasses, a dumb mistress to make love to? What do you lack, gentlemen?

GRIMALDI
Thy mother for a bawd; or, if thou hast
A handsome one, thy sister for a whore;
Without these, do not tell me of your trash,
Or I shall spoil your market.

VITELLI
Old Grimaldi!

GRIMALDI
Zounds, wherefore do we put to sea, or stand
The raging winds, aloft, or upon
The foamy waves, when they rage most; deride
The thunder of the enemy 's shot, board boldly
A merchant's ship for prize, though we behold
The desperate gunner ready to give fire,
And blow the deck up? wherefore shake we off
Those scrupulous rags of charity and conscience,
Invented only to keep churchmen warm,
Or feed the hungry mouths of famish 'd beggars;
But, when we touch the shore, to wallow in
All sensual pleasures?

MASTER
Ay, but, noble captain,
To spare a little for an after-clap,
Were not improvidence.

GRIMALDI
Hang consideration!
When this is spent, is not our ship the same,
Our courage too the same, to fetch in more?
The earth, where it is fertilest, returns not
More than three harvests, while the glorious sun
Posts through the zodiac, and makes up the year:
But the sea, which is our mother, (that embraces
Both the rich Indies in her outstretch'd arms,)
Yields every day a crop, if we dare reap it.
No, no, my mates, let tradesmen think of thrift,
And usurers hoard up; let our expense
Be, as our comings in are, without bounds.
We are the Neptunes of the ocean,
And such as traffic shall pay sacrifice
Of their best lading; I will have this canvass
Your boy wears, lined with tissue, and the cates

You taste, serv'd up in gold: Though we carouse
The tears of orphans in our Greekish wines,
The sighs of undone widows paying for
The music bought to cheer us, ravish 'd virgins
To slavery sold, for coin to feed our riots,
We will have no compunction.

GAZET
Do you hear, sir?
We have paid for our ground.

GRIMALDI
Hum!

GAZET
And hum, too!
For all your big words, get you further off,
And hinder not the prospect of our shop,
Or

GRIMALDI
What will you do?

GAZET
Nothing, sir but pray
Your worship to give me handsel.

GRIMALDI [Seizing him]
By the ears,
Thus, sir, by the ears.

MASTER
Hold, hold!

VITELLI
You'll still be prating.

GRIMALDI
Come, let's be drunk; then each man to his whore.
Slight, how do you look? you had best go find a corner
To pray in, and repent: do, do, and cry;
It will shew fine in pirates.

[Exit.

MASTER
We must follow,
Or he will spend our shares.

BOATSWAIN
I fought for mine.

MASTER
Nor am I so precise but I can drab too:
We will not sit out for our parts.

BOATSWAIN
Agreed.

[Exeunt **MASTER**, **BOATSWAIN** and **SAILORS**.

GAZET
The devil gnaw off his fingers! If he were
In London, among the clubs, up went his heels,
For striking of a prentice. What do you lack?
What do you lack, gentlemen?

1ST TURK
I wonder how the viceroy can endure
The insolence of this fellow.

2ND TURK
He receives profit
From the prizes he brings in; and that excuses
Whatever he commits. Ha! what are these?

[Enter **MUSTAPHA** with **DONUSA** veiled.

1ST TURK
They seem of rank and quality: observe them.

GAZET
What do you lack? see what you please to buy;
Wares of all sorts, most honourable madona.

VITELLI
Peace, sirrah, make no noise; these are not people
To be jested with.

DONUSA
Is this the Christians' custom,
In the venting their commodities?

MUSTAPHA
Yes, best madam.
But you may please to keep your way, here's nothing

But toys and trifles, not worth your observing.

DONUSA
Yes, for variety's sake: pray you, shew us, friend,
The chiefest of your wares.

VITELLI
Your ladyship's servant;
And if, in worth, or title you are more,
My ignorance plead my pardon!

DONUSA
He speaks well.

VITELLI
Take down the looking-glass. Here is a mirror
Steel'd so exactly, neither taking from
Nor flattering the object it returns
To the beholder, that Narcissus might
(And never grow enamour'd of himself)
View his fair feature in't.

DONUSA
Poetical, too!

VITELLI
Here China dishes to serve in a banquet,
Though the voluptuous Persian sat a guest.
Here crystal glasses, such as Ganymede
Did fill with nectar to the Thunderer,
When he drank to Alcides, and received him
In the fellowship of the gods; true to the owners:
Corinthian plate, studded with diamonds,
Conceal'd oft deadly poison; this pure metal
So innocent is, and faithful to the mistress
Or master that possesses it, that, rather
Than hold one drop that's venomous, of itself
It flies in pieces, and deludes the traitor.

DONUSA
How movingly could this fellow treat upon
A worthy subject, that finds such discourse
To grace a trifle!

VITELLI
Here's a picture, madam;
The master-piece of Michael Angelo,
Our great Italian workman; here's another,

So perfect at all parts, that had Pygmalion
Seen this, his prayers had been made to
Venus
To have given it life, and his carved ivory image
By poets ne'er remember'd. They are, indeed,
The rarest beauties of the Christian world,
And no where to be equall'd.

DONUSA
You are partial
In the cause of those you favour; I believe
I instantly could show you one, to theirs
Not much inferior.

VITELLI
With your pardon, madam,
I am incredulous.

DONUSA
Can you match me this?

[Lifts her veil hastily.

VITELLI
What wonder look I on! I'll search above,
And suddenly attend you.

[Exit.

DONUSA
Are you amazed!
I'll bring you to yourself.

[Throws down the glasses.

MUSTAPHA
Ha! what's the matter?

GAZET
My master's ware! Weare undone!
O strange!
A lady to turn roarer, and break glasses!
Tis time to shut up shop then.

MUSTAPHA
You seem moved:
If any language of these Christian dogs
Have called your anger on, in a frown shew it,

And they are dead already.

DONUSA
The offence
Looks not so far. The foolish, paltry fellow,
Shew'd me some trifles, and demanded of me,
For what I valued at so many aspers,
A thousand ducats. I confess he moved me;
Yet I should wrong myself, should such a beggar
Receive least loss from me.

MUSTAPHA
Is it no more?

DONUSA
No, I assure you. Bid him bring his bill
To-morrow to the palace, and enquire
For one Donusa; that word gives him passage
Through all the guard: say, there he shall receive
Full satisfaction. Now, when you please.

MUSTAPHA
I wait you.

[Exeunt **MUSTAPHA** and **DONUSA**

1ST TURK
We must not know them. Let's shift off, and vanish.

[Exeunt **TURKS**.

GAZET
The swine's-pox overtake you! there's a curse
For a Turk, that eats no hog's flesh.

[Re-enter **VITELLI**.

VITELLI
Is she gone?

GAZET
Yes: you may see her handywork.

VITELLI
No matter.
Said she aught else?

GAZET

That you should wait upon her,
And there receive court payment; and, to pass
The guards, she bids you only say you come
To one Donusa.

VITELLI
How! Remove the wares;
Do it without reply. The sultan's niece!
I have heard among the Turks, for any lady
To shew her face bare, argues love, or speaks
Her deadly hatred. What should I fear? my fortune
Is sunk so low, there cannot fall upon me
Aught worth my shunning. I will run the hazard:
She may be a means to free distress'd
Paulina
Or, if offended, at the worst, to die
Is a full period to calamity.

[Exeunt.

SCENE I. A Room in Donusa's Palace

Enter **CARAZIE** and **MANTO**.

CARAZIE
In the name of wonder, Manto, what hath my lady
Done with herself, since yesterday?

MANTO
I know not.
Malicious men report we are all guided
In our affections by a wandering planet:
But such a sudden change in such a person,
May stand for an example, to confirm
Their false assertion.

CARAZIE
She's now pettish, froward;
Music, discourse, observance, tedious to her.

MANTO
She slept not the last night; and yet prevented
The rising sun, in being up before him:
Call'd for a costly bath, then will'd the rooms

Should be perfumed; ransack'd her cabinets
For her choice and richest jewels, and appears now
Like Cynthia in full glory, waited on
By the fairest of the stars.

CARAZIE
Can you guess the reason,
Why the aga of the janizaries, and he
That guards the entrance of the inmost port,
Were call'd before her?

MANTO
They are both her creatures,
And by her grace preferred: but I am ignorant
To what purpose they were sent for.

[Enter **DONUSA**.

CARAZIE
Here she comes,
Full of sad thoughts: we must stand further off.
What a frown was that!

MANTO
Forbear.

CARAZIE
I pity her.

DONUSA
What magic hath transform'd me from myself?
Where is my virgin pride? how have I lost
My boasted freedom? what new fire burns up
My scorched entrails; what unknown desires
Invade, and take possession of my soul,
All virtuous objects vanish'd? I, that have stood
The shock of fierce temptations, stopp'd mine ears
Against all Syren notes lust ever sung,
To draw my bark of chastity (that with wonder
Hath kept a constant and an honour'd course)
Into the gulf of a deserved ill-fame,
Now fall unpitied; and, in a moment,
With mine own hands, dig up a grave to bury
The monumental heap of all my years,
Employ'd in noble actions. O my fate!
But there is no resisting. I obey thee,
Imperious god of love, and willingly
Put mine own fetters on, to grace thy triumph:

'Twere therefore more than cruelty in thee,
To use me like a tyrant. What poor means
Must I make use of now! and flatter such,
To whom, till I betray 'd my liberty,
One gracious look of mine would have erected
An altar to my service! How now,
Manto!
My ever careful woman; and Carazie,
Thou hast been faithful too.

CARAZIE
I dare not call
My life mine own, since it is yours, but gladly
Will part with it, whene'er you shall command me;
And think I fall a martyr, so my death
May give life to your pleasures.

MANTO
But vouchsafe
To let me understand what you desire
Should be effected; I will undertake it,
And curse myself for cowardice, if I paused
To ask the reason why.

DONUSA
I am comforted
In the tender of your service, but shall be
Confirm'd in my full joys, in the performance.
Yet, trust me, I will not impose upon
But what you stand engaged for to a mistress,
Such as I have been to you. All I ask,
Is faith and secrecy.

CARAZIE
Say but you doubt me,
And, to secure you, I'll cut out my tongue;
I am libb'd in the breech already.

MANTO
Do not hinder
Yourself, by these delays.

DONUSA
Thus then I whisper
Mine own shame to you. O that I should blush
To speak what I so much desire to do!
And, further—

[Whispers, and uses vehement action.

MANTO
Is this all?

DONUSA
Think it not base;
Although I know the office undergoes
A coarse construction.

CARAZIE
Coarse! 'tis but procuring;
A smock employment, which has made more knights,
In a country I could name, than twenty years
Of service in the field.

DONUSA
You have my ends.

MANTO
Which say you have arrived at: be not wanting
To yourself, and fear not us.

CARAZIE
I know my burthen;
I'll bear it with delight.

MANTO
Talk not, but do.

[Exeunt **CARAZIE** and **MANTO**

DONUSA
O love, what poor shifts thou dost force us to!

[Exit.

SCENE II. A Court in the Same

Enter **AGA**, **CAPIAGA**, and **JANIZARIES**.

AGA
 She was ever our good mistress, and our maker,
And should we check at a little hazard for her,
We were unthankful.

CAPIAGA
I dare pawn my head,
Tis some disguised minion of the court,
Sent from great Amurath, to learn from her
The viceroy's actions.

AGA
That concerns not us;
His fall may be our rise: whate'er he be,
He passes through my guards.

CAPIAGA
And mine provided
He give the word.

[Enter **VITELLI**.

VITELLI
To faint now, being thus far,
Would argue me of cowardice.

AGA
Stand: the word;
Or, being a Christian, to press thus far,
Forfeits thy life.

VITELLI
Donusa.

AGA
Pass in peace.

[Exeunt **AGA** and **JANIZARIES**.

VITELLI
What a privilege her name bears!
'Tis wondrous strange! If the great officer,
The guardian of the inner port, deny not

CAPIAGA
Thy warrant: Speak, or thou art dead.

VITELLI
Donusa.

CAPIAGA
That protects thee;
Without fear enter. So: discharge the watch.

[Exeunt **VITELLI** and **CAPIAGA**.

SCENE III. An Outer Room in the Same

Enter **CARAZIE** and **MANTO**.

CARAZIE
Though he hath past the aga and chief porter,
This cannot be the man.

MANTO
By her description,
I am sure it is.

CARAZIE
O women, women,
What are you? A great lady dote upon
A haberdasher of small wares!

MANTO
Pish! thou hast none.

CARAZIE
No; if I had, I might have served the turn:
This 'tis to want munition, when a man
Should make a breach, and enter.

[Enter **VITELLI**.

MANTO
Sir, you are welcome:
Think what 'tis to be happy, and possess it.

CARAZIE
Perfume the rooms there, and make way. Let music
With choice notes entertain the man the princess
Now purposes to honour.

VITELLI
I am ravish'd.

[Exeunt.

SCENE IV. A Room of State in the Same

A table set forth, with jewels and bags of money upon it.

Loud music. Enter **DONUSA**, followed by **CARAZIE**, and takes her seal.

DONUSA
Sing o'er the ditty that I last composed
Upon my love-sick passion: suit your voice
To the music that's placed yonder, we shall hear you
With more delight and pleasure.

CARAZIE
I obey you.

[Song.

[During the song, enter **MANTO** and **VITELLI**.

VITELLI
Is not this Tempe, or the blessed shades,
Where innocent spirits reside? or do I dream,
And this a heavenly vision? Howsoever,
It is a sight too glorious to behold,
For such a wretch as I am.

CARAZIE
He is daunted.

MANTO
Speak to him, madam; cheer him up, or you
Destroy what you have built.

CARAZIE
Would I were furnish 'd
With his artillery, and if I stood
Gaping as he does, hang me. [Aside.

[Exeunt **CARAZIE** and **MANTO**.

VITELLI
That I might
Ever dream thus!

[Kneels.

DONUSA
Banish amazement:

You wake; your debtor tells you so, your debtor.
And, to assure you that I am a substance,
And no aerial figure, thus I raise you.
Why do you shake? my soft touch brings no ague;
No biting frost is in this palm; nor are
My looks like to the Gorgon's head, that turn
Men into statues; rather they have power,
Or I have been abused, where they bestow
Their influence, (let me prove it truth in you,
To give to dead men motion.

VITELLI
Can this be?
May I believe my senses? Dare I think
I have a memory, or that you are
That excellent creature that of late disdain'd not
To look on my poor trifles?

DONUSA
I am she.

VITELLI
The owner of that blessed name,
Donusa,
Which, like a potent charm, although pronounced
By my profane, but much unworthier, tongue,
Hath brought me safe to this forbidden place,
Where Christian ne'er yet trod?

DONUSA
I am the same.

VITELLI
And to what end, great lady pardon me,
That I presume to ask, did your command
Command me hither? Or what am I, to whom
You should vouchsafe your favours; nay, your angers?
If any wild or uncollected speech,
Offensively deliver'd, or my doubt
Of your unknown perfections, have displeased you,
You wrong your indignation to pronounce,
Yourself, my sentence: to have seen you only
And to have touch'd that fortune-making hand,
Will with delight weigh down all tortures, that
A flinty hangman's rage could execute,
Or rigid tyranny command with pleasure.

DONUSA

How the abundance of good flowing to thee,
Is wronged in this simplicity! and these bounties,
Which all our Eastern kings have kneeled in vain for,
Do, by thy ignorance, or wilful fear,
Meet with a false construction! Christian, know,
For till thou art mine by a nearer name,
That title, though abhorr'd here, takes not from
Thy entertainment) that 'tis not the fashion
Among the greatest and the fairest dames
This Turkish empire gladly owes and bows to,
To punish where there's no offence, or nourish
Displeasures against those, without whose mercy
They part with all felicity. Prithee, be wise,
And gently understand me; do not force her,
That ne'er knew aught but to command, nor e'er read
The elements of affection, but from such
As gladly sued to her, in the infancy
Of her new-born desires, to be at once
Importunate and immodest.

VITELLI
Did I know,
Great lady, your commands; or, to what purpose
This personated passion tends, (since 'twere
A crime in me deserving death, to think
It is your own,) I should, to make you sport,
Take any shape you please t'impose upon me;
And with joy strive to serve you.

DONUSA
Sport! thou art cruel,
I that thou canst interpret my descent
From my high birth and greatness, but to be
A part, in which I truly act myself:
And I must hold thee for a dull spectator,
If it stir not affection, and invite
Compassion for my sufferings. Be thou taught
By my example, to make satisfaction
For wrongs unjustly offer'd. Willingly
I do confess my fault; I injured thee
In some poor petty trifles; thus I pay for
The trespass I did to thee. Here receive
These bags, stuff'd full of our imperial coin;
Or, if this payment be too light, take here
These gems for which the slavish Indian dives
To the bottom of the main: or, if thou scorn
These as base dross, which take but common minds,
But fancy any honour in my gift,

Which is unbounded as the sultan's power,
And be possest of it.

VITELLI
I am overwhelm'd
With the weight of happiness you throw upon me:
Nor can it fall in my imagination,
What wrong you e'er have done me; and much less
How, like a royal merchant, to return
Your great magnificence.

DONUSA
They are degrees,
Not ends, of my intended favours to thee.
These seeds of bounty I yet scatter on
A glebe I have not tried: but, be thou thankful;
The harvest is to come.

VITELLI
What can be added
To that which I already have received,
I cannot comprehend.

DONUSA
The tender of
Myself. Why dost thou start? and in that gift,
Full restitution of that virgin freedom
Which thou hast robb'd me of. Yet, I profess,
I so far prize the lovely thief that stole it,
That, were it possible thou couldst restore
What thou unwittingly hast ravish'd from me,
I should refuse the present.

VITELLI
How I shake
In my constant resolution! and my flesh,
Rebellious to my better part, now tells me,
As if it were a strong defence of frailty,
A hermit in a desert, trench'd with prayers,
Could not resist this battery.

DONUSA
Thou an Italian,
Nay more, I know't, a natural Venetian,
Such as are courtiers born to please fair ladies,
Yet come thus slowly on!

VITELLI

Excuse me, madam:
What imputation soe'er the world
Is pleased to lay upon us, in myself
I am so innocent, that I know not what 'tis
That I should offer.

DONUSA
By instinct I'll teach thee,
And with such ease as love makes me to ask it.
When a young lady wrings you by the hand, thus,
Or with an amorous touch presses your foot,
Looks babies in your eyes, plays with your locks,
Do not you find, without a tutor's help,
What 'tis she looks for?

VITELLI
I am grown already
Skilful in the mystery.

DONUSA
Or, if thus she kiss you,
Then tastes your lips again

[Kisses him.

VITELLI
That latter blow
Has beat all chaste thoughts from me.

DONUSA
Say, she points to
Some private room the sunbeams never enter,
Provoking dishes passing by, to heighten
Declined appetite, active music ushering
Your fainting steps, the waiters too, as born dumb,
Not daring to look on you.

[Exit, inviting him to follow.

VITELLI
Though the devil
Stood by, and roar'd, I follow: Now I find
That virtue's but a word, and no sure guard,
If set upon by beauty and reward.

[Exit.

Enter **AGA, CAPIAGA, GRIMALDI, MASTER, BOATSWAIN**, and **SAILORS**.

AGA
The devil's in him, I think.

GRIMALDI
Let him be damn'd too.
I'll look on him, though he stared as wild as hell;
Nay, I'll go near to tell him to his teeth,
If he mends not suddenly, and proves more thankful,
We do him too much service. Were't not for shame now,
I could turn honest, and forswear my trade;
Which, next to being truss 'd up at the main yard
By some low country butterbox, I hate
As deadly as I do fasting, or long grace
When meat cools on the table.

CAPIAGA
But take heed;
You know his violent nature.

GRIMALDI
Let his whores
And catamites know't! I understand myself,
And how unmanly 'tis to sit at home,
And rail at us, that run abroad all hazards,
If every week we bring not home new pillage,
For the fatting his seraglio.

[Enter **ASAMBEG, MUSTAPHA**, and **ATTENDANTS**.

AGA
Here he comes.

CAPIAGA
How terrible he looks!

GRIMALDI
To such as fear him.
The viceroy, Asambeg! were he the sultan's self
He'll let us know a reason for his fury;
Or we must take leave, without his allowance,
To be merry with our ignorance.

ASAMBEG

Mahomet's hell
Light on you all! You crouch and cringe now: Where
Was the terror of my just frowns, when you suffer'd
Those thieves of Malta, almost in our harbour,
To board a ship, and bear her safely off,
While you stood idle lookers on?

AGA
The odds
In the men and shipping, and the suddenness
Of their departure, yielding us no leisure
To send forth others to relieve our own,
Deterr'd us, mighty sir.

ASAMBEG
Deterr'd you, cowards!
How durst you only entertain the knowledge
Of what fear was, but in the not performance
Of our command? In me great Amurath spake;
My voice did echo to your ears his thunder
And will'd you, like so many sea-born tritons
Arm'donly with the trumpets of your courage
To swim up to her, and, like remoras
Hanging upon her keel, to stay her flight,
Till rescue, sent from us, had fetch'd you off
You think you're safe now. Who durst but dispute it,
Or make it questionable, if, this moment,
I charged you, from yon hanging cliff, that glasses
His rugged forehead in the neighbouring lake,
To throw yourselves down headlong? or, like faggots,
To fill the ditches of defended forts,
While on your backs we march'd up to the breach?

GRIMALDI
What would not I.

ASAMBEG
Ha!

GRIMALDI
Yet I dare as much
As any of the sultan's boldest sons,
Whose heaven and hell hang on his frown or smile,
His warlike janizaries.

ASAMBEG
Add one syllable more,
Thou dost pronounce upon thyself a sentence

That, earthquake-like, will swallow thee.

GRIMALDI
Let it open,
I'll stand the hazard: those contemned thieves,
But fellow-pirates, sir, the bold Maltese,
Whom with your looks you think to quell, at Rhodes
Laugh'd at great Solyman's anger: and, if treason
Had not delivered them into his power,
He had grown old in glory as in years,
At that so fatal siege; or risen with shame,
His hopes and threats deluded.

ASAMBEG
Our great prophet!
How have I lost my anger and my power!

GRIMALDI
Find it, and use it on thy flatterers,
And not upon thy friends, that dare speak truth.
These knights of Malta, but a handful to
Your armies, that drink rivers up, have stood
Your fury at the height, and with their crosses
Struck pale your horned moons; these men of Malta,
Since I took pay from you, I've met and fought with
Upon advantage too; yet, to speak truth,
By the soul of honour, I have ever found them
As provident to direct, and bold to do,
As any train'd up in your discipline,
Ravish 'd from other nations.

MUSTAPHA
I perceive
The lightning in his fiery looks; the cloud
Is broke already. [Aside.

GRIMALDI
Think not, therefore, sir,
That you alone are giants, and such pigmies
You war upon.

ASAMBEG
Villain! I'll make thee know
Thou hast blasphemed the Othoman power, and safer,
At noonday, might'st have given fire to St. Mark's,
Your proud Venetian temple. Seize upon him:
I am not so near reconciled to him,
To bid him die; that were a benefit

The dog's unworthy of. To our use confiscate
All that he stands possess'd of; let him taste
The misery of want, and his vain riots,
Like to so many walking ghosts, affright him,
Where'er he sets his desperate foot. Who is't
That does command you?

GRIMALDI
Is this the reward
For all my service, and the rape I made
On fair Paulina?

ASAMBEG
Drag him hence: he dies,
That dallies but a minute.

[**GRIMALDI** is dragg'd off, his head covered.

BOATSWAIN
What's become of
Our shares now, master?

MASTER
Would he had been born dumb!
The beggar's cure, patience, is all that's left us.

[Exeunt **MASTER**, **BOATSWAIN**, and **SAILORS**.

MUSTAPHA
'Twas but intemperance of speech, excuse him;
Let me prevail so far. Fame gives him out
For a deserving fellow.

ASAMBEG
At Aleppo,
I durst not press you so far: give me leave
To use my own will, and command in Tunis;
And, if you please, my privacy.

MUSTAPHA
I will see you,
When this high wind's blown o'er.

[Exit.

ASAMBEG
So shall you find me
Ready to do you service. Rage, now leave me;

Stern looks, and all the ceremonious forms
Attending on dread majesty, fly from
Transformed Asambeg. Why should I hug

[Pulls out a key.

So near my heart, what leads me to my prison;
Where she that is inthrall'd, commands her keeper,
And robs me of the fierceness I was born with?
Stout men quake at my frowns, and, in return,
I tremble at her softness. Base Grimaldi
But only named Paulina, and the charm
Had almost choak'd my fury, ere I could
Pronounce his sentence. Would, when first I saw her,
Mine eyes had met with lightning, and, in place
Of hearing her enchanting tongue, the shrieks
Of mandrakes had made music to my slumbers!
For now I only walk a loving dream,
And, but to my dishonour, never wake;
And yet am blind, but when I see the object,
And madly dote on it. Appear, bright spark

[Opens a door; **PAULINA** comes forth.

Of all perfection! any simile
Borrow'd from diamonds, or the fairest stars,
To help me to express how dear I prize
Thy unmatch'd graces, will rise up, and chide me
For poor detraction.

PAULINA
I despise thy flatteries:
Thus spit at them, and scorn them; and being arm'd
In the assurance of my innocent virtue,
I stamp upon all doubts, all fears, all tortures
Thy barbarous cruelty, or, what's worse, thy dotage,
The worthy parent of thy jealousy,
Can shower upon me.

ASAMBEG
 If these bitter taunts
Ravish me from myself, and make me think
My greedy ears receive angelical sounds;
How would this tongue, tuned to a loving note,
Invade, and take possession of my soul,
Which then I durst not call mine own!

PAULINA

Thou art false,
Falser than thy religion. Do but think me
Something above a beast, nay more, a monster
Would fright the sun to look on, and then tell me,
If this base usage can invite affection?
If to be mewed up, and excluded from
Human society; the use of pleasures;
The necessary, not superfluous duties
Of servants, to discharge those offices
I blush to name

ASAMBEG
Of servants! Can you think
That I, that dare not trust the eye of heaven
To look upon your beauties; that deny
Myself the happiness to touch your pureness,
Will e'er consent an eunuch, or bought handmaid,
Shall once approach you? There is something in you
That can work miracles, or I am cozen'd;
Dispose and alter sexes, to my wrong,
In spite of nature. I will be your nurse,
Your woman, your physician, and your fool
Till, with your free consent, which I have vow'd
Never to force, you grace me with a name
That shall supply all these.

PAULINA
What is it?

ASAMBEG
Your husband.

PAULINA
My hangman, when thou pleasest.

ASAMBEG
Thus I guard me
Against your further angers.

[Leads her to the door.

PAULINA
Which shall reach thee,
Though I were in the centre.

[**ASAMBEG** closes the door upon her, and locks it.

ASAMBEG

Such a spirit,
In such a small proportion, I ne'er read of,
Which time must alter. Ravish her I dare not;
The magic that she wears about her neck,
I think, defends her: this devotion paid
To this sweet saint, mistress of my sour pain,
'Tis fit I take mine own rough shape again.

[Exit.

SCENE VI. A Street near Donusa's Palace

Enter **FRANCISCO** and **GAZET**.

FRANCISCO
I think he's lost.

GAZET
'Tis ten to one of that;
I ne'er knew citizen turn courtier yet,
But he lost his credit though he saved himself.
Why, look you, sir, there are so many lobbies,
Out-offices, and dispartations here,
Behind these Turkish hangings, that a
Christian
Hardly gets off but circumcised.

[Enter **VITELLI**, richly habited, **CARAZIE**, and **MANTO**.

FRANCISCO
I am troubled,
Troubled exceedingly. Ha! what are these?

GAZET
One, by his rich suit, should be some
French ambassador:
For his train, I think they are Turks.

FRANCISCO
Peace! be not seen.

CARAZIE
You are now past all the guards, and, undiscover'd,
You may return.

VITELLI

There's for your pains; forget not
My humblest service to the best of ladies.
Manl. Deserve her favour, sir, by making haste
For a second entertainment.

[Exeunt **CARAZIE** and **MANTO**.

VITELLI
Do not doubt me;
I shall not live till then.

GAZET
The train is vanish'd:
They have done him some good office, he's so free
And liberal of his gold. Ha! do I dream,
Or is this mine own natural master?

FRANCISCO
'Tis he:
But strangely metamorphosed. You have made, sir,
A prosperous voyage; heaven grant it be honest,
I shall rejoice then, too.

GAZET
You make him blush,
To talk of honesty: you were but now
In the giving vein, and may think of Gazet,
Your worship's prentice.

VITELLI
There's gold: be thou free too,
And master of my shop, and all the wares
We brought from Venice.

GAZET
Rivo! then.

VITELLI
Dear sir,
This place affords not privacy for discourse;
But I can tell you wonders: my rich habit
Deserves least admiration; there is nothing
That can fall in the compass of your wishes,
Though it were to redeem a thousand slaves
From the Turkish galli'es, or, at home, to erect
Some pious work to shame all hospitals,
But I am master of the means.

FRANCISCO
'Tis strange.

VITELLI
As I walk, I'll tell you more.

GAZET
Pray you, a word, sir;
And then I will put on: I have one boon more.

VITELLI
What is 't? speak freely.

GAZET
Thus then: As I am master
Of your shop and wares, pray you help me to some trucking
With your last she-customer; though she crack my best piece,
I will endure it with patience.

VITELLI
Leave your prating.

GAZET
I may: you have been doing; we will do too.

FRANCISCO
I am amazed, yet will not blame nor chide you,
Till you inform me further: yet must say,
They steer not the right course, nor traffic well,
That seek a passage to reach heaven through hell.

[Exeunt.

ACT III

SCENE I. A Room in Donusa's Palace

Enter **DONUSA** and **MANTO**.

DONUSA
When said he would come again?

MANTO
He swore,
Short minutes should be tedious ages to him,
Until the tender of his second service;

So much he seemed transported with the first.

DONUSA
I'm sure I was. I charge thee, Manto, tell me,
By all my favours, and my bounties, truly,
Whether thou art a virgin, or, like me,
Hast forfeited that name?

MANTO
A virgin, madam,
At my years! being a waiting-woman, and in court too!
That were miraculous. I so long since lost
That barren burthen, I almost forget
That ever I was one.

DONUSA
And could thy friends
Head in thy face, thy maidenhead gone, that thou
Had'st parted with it?

MANTO
No, indeed: I past
For current many years after, till, by fortune,
Long and continued practice in the sport
Slew up my deck; a husband then was found out
By my indulgent father, and to the world
All was made whole again. What need you fear, then,
That, at your pleasure, may repair your honour,
Durst any envious or malicious tongue
Presume to taint it?

[Enter **CARAZIE**.

DONUSA
How now?

CARAZIE
Madam, the basha dumbly desires access.

DONUSA
If it had been
My neat Italian, thou hadst met my wishes.
Tell him we would be private.

CARAZIE
So I did,
But he is much importunate.

MANTO
Best despatch him:
His lingering here else will deter the other
From making his approach.

DONUSA
His entertainment
Shall not invite a second visit. Go;
Say we are pleased.

[Enter **MUSTAPHA**.

MUSTAPHA
All happiness

DONUSA
Be sudden.
'Twas saucy rudeness in you, sir, to press
On my retirements; but ridiculous folly
To waste the time, that might be better spent,
In complimental wishes.

CARAZIE
There's a cooling
For his hot encounter! [Aside.

DONUSA
Come you here to stare?
If you have lost your tongue, and use of speech,
Resign your government; there's a mute's place void
In my uncle's court, I hear; and you may work me,
To write for your preferment.

MUSTAPHA
This is strange!
I know not, madam, what neglect of mine
Has call'd this scorn upon me.

DONUSA
To the purpose
My will's a reason, and we stand not bound
To yield account to you.

MUSTAPHA
Not of your angers:
But with erected ears I should hear from you
The story of your good opinion of me,
Confirm'd by love and favours.

DONUSA
How deserved?
I have considered you from head to foot,
And can find nothing in that wainscot face,
That can teach me to dote; nor am I taken
With your grim aspect, or tadpole-like complexion.
Those scars you glory in, I fear to look on;
And had much rather hear a merry tale,
Than all your battles won with blood and sweat,
Though you belch forth the stink too in the service,
And swear by your mustachios all is true.
You are yet too rough for me: purge and; take physic,
Purchase perfumers, get me some French tailor
To new-create you; the first shape you were made with
Is quite worn out: let your barber wash your face too,
You look yet like a bugbear to fright children;
Till when I take my leave. Wait me, Carazie.

[Exeunt **DONUSA** and **CARAZIE**.

MUSTAPHA
Stay you, my lady's cabinet-key.

[Seizes **MANTO**.

MANTO
How's this, sir?

MUSTAPHA
Stay, and stand quietly, or you shall fall else,
Not to firk your belly up, flounder-like, but never
To rise again. Offer but to unlock
These doors that stop your fugitive tongue, (observe me,)
And, by my fury, I'll fix there this bolt

[Draws his scimitar.

To bar thy speech for ever. So! be safe now;
And but resolve me, not of what I doubt,
But bring assurance to a thing believed,
Thou makest thyself a fortune; not depending
On the uncertain favours of a mistress,
But art thyself one. I'll not so far question
My judgment and observance, as to ask
Why I am slighted and contemn'd; but in
Whose favour it is done? I, that have read
The copious volume of all women's falsehood,

Commented on by the heart-breaking groans
Of abused lovers; all the doubts wash'd off
With fruitless tears, the spider's cobweb veil
Of arguments alleged in their defence,
Blown off with sighs of desperate men, and, they
Appearing in their full deformity;
Know that some other hath displanted me,
With her dishonour. Has she given it up?
Confirm it in two syllables.

MANTO
She has.

MUSTAPHA
I cherish thy confession thus, and thus;

[Gives her jewels.

Be mine. Again I court thee thus, and thus:
Now prove but constant to my ends.

MANTO
By all

MUSTAPHA
Enough; I dare not doubt thee.
O land crocodiles,
Made of Egyptian slime, accursed women!
But 'tis no time to rail come, my best Manto.

[Exeunt.

SCENE II. A Street

Enter **VITELLI** and **FRANCISCO**.

VITELLI
Sir, as you are my confessor, you stand bound
Not to reveal whatever I discover
In that religious way; nor dare I doubt you.
Let it suffice you have made me see my follies,
And wrought, perhaps, compunction; for I would not
Appear an hypocrite. But, when you impose
A penance on me beyond flesh and blood
To undergo, you must instruct me how
To put off the condition of a man:

Or, if not pardon, at the least, excuse
My disobedience. Yet, despair not, sir;
For, though I take mine own way, I shall do
Something that may hereafter, to my glory,
Speak me your scholar.

FRANCISCO
I enjoin you not
To go, but send.

VITELLI
That were a petty trial;
Not worth one, so long taught, and exercised,
Under so grave a master. Reverend Francisco,
My friend, my father, in that word, my all!
Rest confident you shall hear something of me,
That will redeem me in your good opinion;
Or judge me lost for ever. Send Gazet
(She shall give order that he may have entrance)
To acquaint you with my fortunes.

[Exit.

FRANCISCO
Go, and prosper.
Holy saints guide and strengthen thee! however,
As thy endeavours are, so may they find
Gracious acceptance.

[Enter **GAZET**, and **GRIMALDI** in rags.

GAZET
Now, you do not roar, sir;
You speak not tempests, nor take ear-rent from
A poor shop-keeper. Do you remember that, sir?
I wear your marks here still.

FRANCISCO
Can this be possible?
All wonders are not ceased, then.

GRIMALDI
Do, abuse me,
Spit on me. spurn me, pull me by the nose,
Thrust out these fiery eyes, that yesterday
Would have look'd thee dead.

GAZET

O save me, sir!

GRIMALDI
Fear nothing.
I am tame and quiet; there's no wrong can force me
To remember what I was. I have forgot
I e'er had ireful fierceness, a steel'd heart,
Insensible of compassion to others;
Nor is it fit that I should think myself
Worth mine own pity. Oh!

FRANCISCO
Grows this dejection
From his disgrace, do you say?

GAZET
Why, he's cashier'd, sir;
His ships, his goods, his livery-punks, confiscate:
And there is such a punishment laid upon him!
The miserable rogue must steal no more,
Nor drink, nor drab.

FRANCISCO
Does that torment him?

GAZET
O, sir,
Should the state take order to bar men of acres
From these two laudable recreations,
Drinking and whoring, how should panders purchase,
Or thrifty whores build hospitals? 'Slid! if I,
That, since I am made free, may write myself
A city gallant, should forfeit two such charters,
I should be stoned to death, and ne'er be pitied
By the liveries of those companies.

FRANCISCO
You'll be whipt, sir,
If you bridle not your tongue. Haste to the palace,
Your master looks for you.

GAZET
My quondam master.
Rich sons forget they ever had poor fathers;
In servants 'tis more pardonable: as a companion,
Or so, I may consent: but, is there hope, sir,
He has got me a good chap woman? pray you, write
A word or two in my behalf.

FRANCISCO
Out, rascal!

GAZET
I feel some insurrections.

FRANCISCO
Hence!

GAZET
I vanish.

[Exit.

GRIMALDI
Why should I study a defence or comfort,
In whom black guilt and misery, if balanced,
I know not which would turn the scale? look upward
I dare not; for, should it but be believed
That I, died deep in hell's most horrid colours,
Should dare to hope for mercy, it would leave
No check or feeling in men innocent,
To catch at sins the devil ne'er taught mankind yet.
No! I must downward, downward; though repentance
Could borrow all the glorious wings of grace,
My mountainous weight of sins would crack their pinions,
And sink them to hell with me.

FRANCISCO
Dreadful! Hear me,
Thou miserable man.

GRIMALDI
Good sir, deny not
But that there is no punishment beyond
Damnation.

[Enter **MASTER** and **BOATSWAIN**.

MASTER
Yonder he is; I pity him.

BOATSWAIN
Take comfort, captain; we live still to serve you.

GRIMALDI
Serve me! I am a devil already: leave me

Stand further off, you are blasted else! I have heard
Schoolmen affirm man's body is composed
Of the four elements; and, as in league together
They nourish life, so each of them affords
Liberty to the soul, when it grows weary
Of this fleshy prison. Which shall I make choice of?
The fire? no; I shall feel that hereafter;
The earth will not receive me. Should some whirlwind
Snatch me into the air, and I hang there,
Perpetual plagues would dwell upon the earth;
And those superior bodies, that pour down
Their cheerful influence, deny to pass it,
Through those vast regions I have infected.
The sea? ay, that is justice: there I plough'd up
Mischief as deep as hell: there, there, I'll hide
This cursed lump of clay. May it turn rocks,
Where plummet's weight could never reach the sands,
And grind the ribs of all such barks as press
The ocean's breast in my unlawful course!
I haste then to thee; let thy ravenous womb,
Whom all things else deny, be now my tomb!

[Exit.

MASTER
Follow him, and restrain him.

[Exit **BOATSWAIN**.

FRANCISCO
Let this stand
For an example to you. I'll provide
A lodging for him, and provide such cures
To his wounded conscience, as heaven hath lent me.
He's now my second care; and my profession
Binds me to teach the desperate to repent,
As far as to confirm the innocent.

[Exeunt.

SCENE III. A Room in Asambeg's Palace

Enter **ASAMBEG**, **MUSTAPHA**, **AGA**, and **CAPIAGA**.

ASAMBEG
Your pleasure?

MUSTAPHA
'Twill exact your private ear;
And, when you have received it, you will think
Too many know it.

ASAMBEG
Leave the room; but be
Within our call.

[Exeunt **AGA**, and **CAPIAGA**.

Now, sir, what burning secret
(With which, it seems, you are turn'd cinders) bring you,
To quench in my advice or power?

MUSTAPHA
The fire
Will rather reach you.

ASAMBEG
Me!

MUSTAPHA
And consume both;
For 'tis impossible to be put out,
But with the blood of those that kindle it:
And yet one vial of it is so precious,
In being borrow'd from the Othoman spring,
That better 'tis, I think, both we should perish,
Than prove the desperate means that must restrain it
From spreading further.

ASAMBEG
To the point, and quickly:
These winding circumstances in relations,
Seldom environ truth.

MUSTAPHA
Truth, Asambeg!

ASAMBEG
Truth, Mustapha. I said it, and add more,
You touch upon a string that, to my ear,
Does sound Donusa.

MUSTAPHA
You then understand

Who 'tis I aim at.

ASAMBEG
Take heed, Mustapha;
Remember what she is, and whose we are:
'Tis her neglect, perhaps, that you complain of;
And, should you practise to revenge her scorn,
With any plot to taint her in her honour,

MUSTAPHA
Hear me.

ASAMBEG
I will be heard first, there's no tongue
A subject owes, that shall out-thunder mine.

MUSTAPHA
Well, take your way.

ASAMBEG
I then again repeat it;
If Mustapha dares with malicious breath,
On jealous suppositions, presume
To blast the blossom of Donusa's fame,
Because he is denied a happiness
Which men of equal, nay, of more desert,
Have sued in vain for

MUSTAPHA
More!

ASAMBEG
More. 'Twas I spake it.
The basha of Natolia and myself
Were rivals for her; either of us brought
More victories, more trophies, to plead for us
To our great master, than you dare lay claim to;
Yet still, by his allowance, she was left
To her election: each of us owed nature
As much for outward form and inward worth,
To make way for us to her grace and favour,
As you brought with you. We were heard, repulsed;
Yet thought it no dishonour to sit down
With the disgrace, if not to force affection
May merit such a name.

MUSTAPHA
Have you done yet?

ASAMBEG

Be, therefore, more than sure the ground on which
You raise your accusation, may admit
No undermining of defence in her:
For if, with pregnant and apparent proofs,
Such as may force a judge, more than inclined,
Or partial in her cause, to swear her guilty,
You win not me to set off your belief;
Neither our ancient friendship, nor the rites
Of sacred hospitality, to which
I would not offer violence, shall protect you:
Now, when you please.

MUSTAPHA

I will not dwell upon
Much circumstance; yet cannot but profess,
With the assurance of a loyalty
Equal to yours, the reverence I owe
The sultan, and all such his blood makes sacred;
That there is not a vein of mine, which yet is
Unemptied in his service, but this moment
Should freely open, so it might wash off
The stains of her dishonour. Could you think,
Or, though you saw it, credit your own eyes,
That she, the wonder and amazement of
Her sex, the pride and glory of the empire,
That hath disdain'd you, slighted me, and boasted
A frozen coldness, which no appetite
Or height of blood could thaw; should now so far
Be hurried with the violence of her lust,
As, in it burying her high birth, and fame,
Basely descend to fill a Christian's arms;
And to him yield her virgin honour up,
Nay, sue to him to take it?

ASAMBEG

A Christian!

MUSTAPHA

Temper
Your admiration: and what Christian, think you?
No prince disguised, no man of mark, nor honour;
No daring undertaker in our service,
But one, whose lips her foot should scorn to touch;
A poor mechanic pedlar.

ASAMBEG

He!

MUSTAPHA
Nay, more;
Whom do you think she made her scout, nay bawd,
To find him out, but me? What place make choice of
To wallow in her foul and loathsome pleasures,
But in the palace? Who the instruments
Of close conveyance, but the captain of
Your guard, the aga, and that man of trust,
The warden of the inmost port? I'll prove this:
And, though I fail to shew her in the act,
Glued like a neighing gennet to her stallion,
Your incredulity shall be convinced
With proofs I blush to think on.

ASAMBEG
Never yet
This flesh felt such a fever. By the life
And fortune of great Amurath, should our prophet
(Whose name I bow to) in a vision speak this,
Twould make me doubtful of my faith!
Lead on;
And, when my eyes and ears are, like yours, guilty,
My rage shall then appear; for I will do
Something but what, I am not yet determin'd.

[Exeunt.

SCENE IV. An Outer Room in Donusa's Palace

Enter **CARAZIE**, **MANTO**, and **GAZET** gaily dressed.

CARAZIE
They are private to their wishes?

MANTO
Doubt it not.

GAZET
A pretty structure this! a court do you call it?
Vaulted and arch'd! O, here has been old jumbling
Behind this arras.

CARAZIE
Prithee let's have some sport

With this fresh codshead.

MANTO
I am out of tune,
But do as you please. My conscience! tush! the hope
Of liberty throws that burthen off; I must
Go watch, and make discovery.

[Aside, and exit.

CARAZIE
He is musing,
And will talk to himself; he cannot hold:
The poor fool's ravish 'd.

GAZET
I am in my master's clothes,
They fit me to a hair too; let but any
Indifferent gamester measure us inch by inch,
Or weigh us by the standard, I may pass:
I have been proved and proved again true metal.

CARAZIE
How he surveys himself!

GAZET
I have heard, that some
Have fooled themselves at court into good fortunes,
That never hoped to thrive by wit in the city,
Or honesty in the country. If I do not
Make the best laugh at me, I'll weep for myself,
If they give me hearing: 'tis resolved I'll try
What may be done. By your favour, sir, I pray you,
Were you born a courtier?

CARAZIE
No, sir; why do you ask?

GAZET
Because I thought that none could be preferred,
But such as were begot there.

CARAZIE
O, sir! many;
And, howsoe'er you are a citizen born,
Yet if your mother were a handsome woman,
And ever long'd to see a masque at court,
It is an even lay, but that you had

A courtier to your father; and I think so,
You bear yourself so sprightly.

GAZET
It may be;
But pray you, sir, had I such an itch upon me
To change my copy, is there hope a place
May be had here for money?

CARAZIE
Not without it,
That I dare warrant you.

GAZET
I have a pretty stock,
And would not have my good parts undiscover'd:
What places of credit are there?

CARAZIE
There's your beglerbeg.

GAZET
By no means that; it comes too near the beggar,
And most prove so, that come there.

CARAZIE
Or your sanzacke.

GAZET
Sauce-jack! fie, none of that.

CARAZIE
Your chiaus.

GAZET
Nor that.

CARAZIE
Chief gardener.

GAZET
Out upon't!
Twill put me in mind my mother was an herb-woman.
What is your place, I pray you?

CARAZIE
Sir, an eunuch.

GAZET
An eunuch! very fine, i' faith; an eunuch!
And what are your employments?

CARAZIE
Neat and easy:
In the day, I wait on my lady when she eats,
Carry her pantofles, bear up her train;
Sing her asleep at night, and, when she pleases,
I am her bedfellow.

GAZET
How! her bedfellow?
And lie with her?

CARAZIE
Yes, and lie with her.

GAZET
O rare!
I'll be an eunuch, though I sell my shop for't,
And all my wares.

CARAZIE
It is but parting with
A precious stone or two: I know the price on't.

GAZET
I'll part with all my stones; and when I am
An eunuch, I'll so toss and to use the ladies
Pray you help me to a chapman.

CARAZIE
The court surgeon
Shall do you that favour.

GAZET
I am made! an eunuch I

[Enter **MANTO**.

MANTO
Carazie, quit the room.

CARAZIE
Come, sir; we'll treat of
Your business further.

GAZET
Excellent! an eunuch!

[Exeunt.

Enter **DONUSA** and **VITELLI**.

VITELLI
Leave me, or I am lost again: no prayers,
No penitence, can redeem me.

DONUSA
Am I grown
Old or deform'd since yesterday?

VITELLI
You are still,
(Although the sating of your lust hath sullied
The immaculate whiteness of your virgin beauties,)
Too fair for me to look on: and, though pureness,
The sword with which you ever fought and conquer'd,
Is ravish'd from you by unchaste desires,
You are too strong for flesh and blood to treat with,
Though iron grates were interpos'd between us,
To warrant me from treason.

DONUSA
Whom do you fear?

VITELLI
That human frailty I took from my mother,
That, as my youth increased, grew stronger on me;
That still pursues me, and, though once recover'd,
In scorn of reason, and, what's more, religion,
Again seeks to betray me.

DONUSA
If you mean, sir,
To my embraces, you turn rebel to
The laws of nature, the great queen and mother
Of all productions, and deny allegiance,
Where you stand bound to pay it.

VITELLI

I will stop
Mine ears against these charms, which, if Ulysses
Could live again, and hear this second Syren,
Though bound with cables to his mast, his ship too
Fasten'd with all her anchors, this enchantment
Would force him, in despite of all resistance,
To leap into the sea, and follow her;
Although destruction, with outstretch'd arms,
Stood ready to receive him.

DONUSA
Gentle sir,
Though you deny to hear me, yet vouchsafe
To look upon me: though I use no language,
The grief for this unkind repulse will print
Such a dumb eloquence upon my face,
As will not only plead but prevail for me.

VITELLI
I am a coward. I will see and hear you,
The trial, else, is nothing; nor the conquest,
My temperance shall crown me with hereafter,
Worthy to be remember'd. Up, my virtue!
And holy thoughts and resolutions arm me
Against this fierce temptation! give me voice
Tuned to a zealous anger, to express
At what an over-value I have purchased
The wanton treasure of your virgin bounties;
That, in their false fruition, heap upon me
Despair and horror. That I could with that ease
Redeem my forfeit innocence, or cast up
The poison I received into my entrails,
From the alluring cup of your enticements,
As now I do deliver back the price

[Returns the jewels.

And salary of your lust! or thus unclothe me
Of sin's gay trappings, the proud livery

[Throws off his cloak and doublet.

Of wicked pleasure, which but worn and heated
With the fire of entertainment and consent,
Like to Alcides' fatal shirt, tears off
Our flesh and reputation both together,
Leaving our ulcerous follies bare and open

To all malicious censure!

DONUSA
You must grant,
If you hold that a loss to you, mine equals,
If not transcends it. If you then first tasted
That poison, as you call it, I brought with me
A palate unacquainted with the relish
Of those delights, which most, as I have heard,
Greedily swallow; and then the offence,
If my opinion may be believed,
Is not so great: howe'er, the wrong no more,
Than if Hippolitus and the virgin huntress
Should meet and kiss together.

VITELLI
What defences
Can lust raise to maintain a precipice

[Enter **ASAMBERG** and **MUSTAPHA**, above.

To the abyss of looseness! but affords not
The least stair, or the fastening of one foot,
To re-ascend that glorious height we fell from.

MUSTAPHA
By Mahomet, she courts him!

[**DONUSA** kneels.

ASAMBEG
Nay, kneels to him!
Observe, the scornful villain turns away too,
As glorying in his conquest.

DONUSA
Are you marble?
If Christians have mothers, sure they share in
The tigress' fierceness; for, if you were owner
Of human pity, you could not endure
A princess to kneel to you, or look on
These falling tears which hardest rocks would soften,
And yet remain unmoved. Did you but give me
A taste of happiness in your embraces,
That the remembrance of the sweetness of it
Might leave perpetual bitterness behind it?
Or shew'd me what it was to be a wife,
To live a widow ever?

ASAMBEG
She has confest it!
Seize on him, villains.

[Enter **CAPIAGA** and **AGA**, with **JANIZARIES**.

O the Furies!

[Exeunt **ASAMBEG** and **MUSTAPHA** above.

DONUSA
How!
Are we betray'd?

VITELLI
The better; I expected
A Turkish faith.

DONUSA
Who am I, that you dare this?
'Tis I that do command you to forbear
A touch of violence.

AGA
We, already, madam,
Have satisfied your pleasure further than
We know to answer it.

CAPIAGA
Would we were well off!
We stand too far engaged, I fear.

DONUSA
For us?

We'll bring you safe off: who dares contradict
What is our pleasure?

[Re-enter **ASAMBEG** and **MUSTAPHA**, below.

ASAMBEG
Spurn the dog to prison.
I'll answer you anon.

VITELLI
What punishment
Soe'er I undergo, I am still a Christian.

[Exit **GUARD** with **VITELLI**.

DONUSA
What bold presumption's this?
Under what law
Am I to fall, that set my foot upon
Your statutes and decrees?

MUSTAPHA
The crime committed,
Our Alcoran calls death.

DONUSA
Tush! who is here,
That is not Amurath's slave, and so, unfit
To sit a judge upon his blood?

ASAMBEG
You have lost,
And shamed the privilege of it; robb'd me too
Of my soul, my understanding, to behold
Your base unworthy fall from your high virtue.
Don, I do appeal to Amurath.

ASAMBEG
We will offer
No violence to your person, till we know
His sacred pleasure; till when, under guard
You shall continue here.

DONUSA
Shall!

ASAMBEG
I have said it.

DONUSA
We shall remember this.

ASAMBEG
It ill becomes
Such as are guilty, to deliver threats
Against the innocent.

[The **GUARD** leads **DONUSA**.

I could tear this flesh now,

But 'tis in vain; nor must I talk, but do.
Provide a well-mann'd galley for Constantinople:
Such sad news never came to our great master.
As he directs, we must proceed, and know
No will but his, to whom what's ours we owe.

[Exeunt.

SCENE I. A Room in Grimaldi's House

Enter **MASTER** and **BOATSWAIN**.

MASTER
He does begin to eat?

BOATSWAIN
A little, master;
But our best hope for his recovery is, that
His raving leaves him; and those dreadful words,
Damnation and despair, with which he ever
Ended all his discourses, are forgotten.

MASTER
This stranger is a most religious man sure;
And I am doubtful, whether his charity
In the relieving of our wants, or care
To cure the wounded conscience of Grimaldi,
Deserves more admiration.

BOATSWAIN
Can you guess
What the reason should be, that we never mention
The church, or the high altar, but his melancholy
Grows and increases on him?

MASTER
I have heard him,
When he gloried to profess himself an atheist,
Talk often, and with much delight and boasting,
Of a rude prank he did ere he turn'd pirate
The memory of which, as it appears,
Lies heavy on him,

BOATSWAIN

Pray you, let me understand it.

MASTER
Upon a solemn day, when the whole city
Join'd in devotion, and with barefoot steps
Passed to St. Mark's, the duke, and the whole signiory,
Helping to perfect the religious pomp
With which they were received; when all men else
Were full of tears, and groan'd beneath the weight
Of past offences, of whose heavy burthen
They came to be absolved and freed; our captain,
Whether in scorn of those so pious rites
He had no feeling of, or else drawn to it
Out of a wanton, irreligious madness,
(I know not which,) ran to the holy man,
As he was doing of the work of grace,
And snatching from his hands the sanctified means,
Dash'd it upon the pavement.

BOATSWAIN
How escaped he,
It being a deed deserving death with torture?

MASTER
The general amazement of the people
Gave him leave to quit the temple, and a gondola,
Prepared, it seems, before, brought him aboard;
Since which he ne'er saw Venice. The remembrance
Of this, it seems, torments him; aggravated
With a strong belief he cannot receive pardon
For this foul fact, but from his hands, against whom
It was committed.

BOATSWAIN
And what course intends
His heavenly physician, reverend Francisco,
To beat down this opinion?

MASTER
He promised
To use some holy and religious fineness,
To this good end; and, in the meantime, charged me
To keep him dark, and to admit no visitants;
But on no terms to cross him. Here he comes.

[Enter **GRIMALDI**, with a book.

GRIMALDI

For theft, he that restores treble the value,
Makes satisfaction; and, for want of means
To do so, as a slave must serve it out,
Till he hath made full payment. There's hope left here.
Oh! with what willingness would I give up
My liberty to those that I have pillaged;
And wish the numbers of my years, though wasted
In the most sordid slavery, might equal
The rapines I have made; till, with one voice,
My patient sufferings might exact, from my
Most cruel creditors, a full remission,
An eye's loss with an eye, limb's with a limb:
A sad account! yet, to find peace within here,
Though all such as I have maim'd and dismember'd
In drunken quarrels, or o'ercome with rage,
When they were given up to my power, stood here now,
And cried for restitution; to appease them,
I would do a bloody justice on myself:
Pull out these eyes, that guided me to ravish
Their sight from others; lop these legs, that bore me
To barbarous violence; with this hand cut off
This instrument of wrong, till nought were left me
But this poor bleeding limbless trunk, which gladly
I would divide among them. Ha! what think I

[Enter **FRANCISCO** in a cope, like a Bishop.

Of petty forfeitures! In this reverend habit,
All that I am turn'd into eyes, I look on
A deed of mine so fiend-like, that repentance,
Though with my tears I taught the sea new tides,
Can never wash off: all my thefts, my rapes,
Are venial trespasses, compared to what
I offer'd to that shape, and in a place too,
Where I stood bound to kneel to 't.

[Kneels.

FRANCISCO
'Tis forgiven:
I with his tongue, whom, in these sacred vestments,
With impure hands thou didst offend, pronounce it.
I bring peace to thee; see that thou deserve it
In thy fair life hereafter.

GRIMALDI
Can it be!
Dare I believe this vision, or hope

A pardon e'er may find me?

FRANCISCO
Purchase it
By zealous undertakings, and no more
'Twill be remembered.

GRIMALDI
What celestial balm

[Rises.

I feel now pour'd into my wounded conscience!
What penance is there I'll not undergo,
Though ne'er so sharp and rugged, with more pleasure
Than flesh and blood e'er tasted! show me true Sorrow,
Arm'd with an iron whip, and I will meet
The stripes she brings along with her, as if
They were the gentle touches of a hand
That comes to cure me. Can good deeds redeem me?
I will rise up a wonder to the world,
When I have given strong proofs how I am alter'd.
I, that have sold such as profess 'd the faith
That I was born in, to captivity,
Will make their number equal, that I shall
Deliver from the oar; and win as many
By the clearness of my actions, to look on
Their misbelief, and loath it. I will be
A convoy for all merchants; and thought worthy
To be reported to the world, hereafter,
The child of your devotion; nurs'd up,
And made strong by your charity, to break through
All dangers hell can bring forth to oppose me.
Nor am I, though my fortunes were thought desperate,
Now you have reconciled me to myself,
So void of worldly means, but, in despite
Of the proud viceroy's wrongs, I can do something
To witness of my change: when you please, try me,
And I will perfect what you shall enjoin me,
Or fall a joyful martyr.

FRANCISCO
You will reap
The comfort of it; live yet undiscover'd,
And with your holy meditations strengthen.
Your Christian resolution: ere long,
You shall hear further from me.

[Exit.

GRIMALDI
I'll attend
All your commands with patience; come my mates,
I hitherto have lived an ill example,
And, as your captain, led you on to mischief;
But now will truly labour, that good men
May say hereafter of me, to my glory,
(Let but my power and means hand with my will,)
His good endeavours did weigh down his ill.

[Exeunt.

[Re-enter **FRANCISCO**, in his usual habit.

FRANCISCO
This penitence is not counterfeit: howsoever,
Good actions are in themselves rewarded.
My travail's to meet with a double crown.
If that Vitelli come off safe, and prove
Himself the master of his wild affections

[Enter **GAZET**.

O, I shall have intelligence; how now,
Gazet,
Why these sad looks and tears?

GAZET
Tears, sir! I have lost
My worthy master. Your rich heir seems to mourn for
A miserable father, your young widow,
Following a bed-rid husband to his grave,
Would have her neighbours think she cries and roars,
That she must part with such a good man
Do-nothing;
When 'tis, because he stays so long above ground,
And hinders a rich suitor. All's come out, sir.
We are smok'd for being coney-catchers: my master
Is put in prison; his she-customer
Is under guard too; these are things to weep for:
But mine own loss consider 'd, and what a fortune
I have had, as they say, snatch'd out of my chops,
Would make a man run mad.

FRANCISCO
I scarce have leisure,

I am so wholly taken up with sorrow
For my loved pupil, to enquire thy fate;
Yet I will hear it.

GAZET
Why, sir, I had bought a place,
A place of credit too, an I had gone through with it;
I should have been made an eunuch: there was honour
For a late poor prentice! when, upon the sudden,
There was such a hurly-burly in the court,
That I was glad to run away, and carry
The price of my office with me.

FRANCISCO
Is that all?
You have made a saving voyage: we must think now,
Though not to free, to comfort sad Vitelli;
My grieved soul suffers for him.

GAZET
I am sad too;
But had I been an eunuch

FRANCISCO
Think not on it.

[Exeunt.

SCENE II. A Hall in Asambeg's Palace

Enter **ASAMBEG**; he unlocks a door, and **PAULINA** comes forth.

ASAMBEG
 Be your own guard: obsequiousness and service
Shall win you to be mine. Of all restraint
For ever take your leave, no threats shall awe you,
No jealous doubts of mine disturb your freedom,
No fee'd spies wait upon your steps: your virtue,
And due consideration in yourself
Of what is noble, are the faithful helps
I leave you, as supporters, to defend you
From falling basely.

PAULINA
This is wondrous strange:
Whence flows this alteration?

ASAMBEG

From true judgment;
And strong assurance, neither grates of iron,
Hemm'd in with walls of brass, strict guards, high birth,
The forfeiture of honour, nor the fear
Of infamy or punishment, can stay
A woman slaved to appetite, from being
False, and unworthy.

PAULINA

You are grown satirical
Against our sex. Why, sir, I durst produce
Myself in our defence, and from you challenge
A testimony that's not to be denied,
All fall not under this unequal censure.
I, that have stood your flatteries, your threats,
Borne up against your fierce temptations; scorn 'd
The cruel means you practised to supplant me,
Having no arms to help me to hold out,
But love of piety, and constant goodness;
If you are unconfirm'd, dare again boldly,
Enter into the lists, and combat with
All opposites man's malice can bring forth
To shake me in my chastity, built upon
The rock of my religion.

ASAMBEG

I do wish
I could believe you; but, when I shall shew you
A most incredible example of
Your frailty, in a princess, sued and sought to
By men of worth, of rank, of eminence; courted
By happiness itself, and her cold temper
Approved by many years; yet she to fall,
Fall from herself, her glories', nay, her safety,
Into a gulf of shame and black despair; '
I think you'll doubt yourself, or, in beholding
Her punishment, for ever be deterr'd
From yielding basely.

PAULINA

I would see this wonder;
Tis, sir, my first petition.

ASAMBEG

And thus granted:
Above, you shall observe all.

[Exit **PAULINA**.

[Enter **MUSTAPHA**.

MUSTAPHA
Sir, I sought you,
And must relate a wonder. Since I studied,
And knew what man was, I was never witness
Of such invincible fortitude as this Christian
Shews in his sufferings: all the torments that
We could present him with, to fright his constancy,
Confirm 'd, not shook it; and those heavy chains,
That eat into his flesh, appear 'd to him
Like bracelets made of some loved mistress' hairs,
We kiss in the remembrance of her favours.
I am strangely taken with it, and have lost
Much of my fury.

ASAMBEG
Had he suffer'd poorly,
It had call'd on my contempt; but manly patience,
And all-commanding virtue, wins upon
An enemy. I shall think upon him. Ha!

[Enter **AGA**, with a black box.

So soon return'd! This speed pleads in excuse
Of your late fault, which I no more remember.
What's the grand signior's pleasure?

AGA
'Tis enclosed here.
The box too that contains it may inform you
How he stands affected: I am trusted with
Nothing but this, On forfeit of your head,
She must have a speedy trial.

ASAMBEG
Bring her in
In black, as to her funeral:

[Exit **AGA**.

'Tis the colour
Her fault wills her to wear, and which, in justice,
I dare not pity. Sit, and take your place:
However in her life she has degenerated,

May she die nobly, and in that confirm
Her greatness and high blood!

[Solemn music.

[Re-enter the **AGA**, with the **CAPIAGA** leading in **DONUSA** in black, her train borne up by **CARAZIE** and **MANTO**. A **GUARD** attending. **PAULINA** enters above.

MUSTAPHA
I now could melt
But soft compassion leave me.

MANTO
I am affrighted
With this dismal preparation. Should the enjoying
Of loose desires find ever such conclusions,
All women would be Vestals.

DONUSA
That you clothe me
In this sad livery of death, assures me
Your sentence is gone out before, and I
Too late am call'd for, in my guilty cause
To use qualification or excuse
Yet must I not part so with mine own strengths,
But borrow, from my modesty, boldness, to
Enquire by whose authority you sit
My judges, and whose warrant digs my grave
In the frowns you dart against my life?

ASAMBEG
See here,
This fatal sign and warrant! This, brought to
A general, fighting in the head of his
Victorious troops, ravishes from his hand
His even then conquering sword; this, shewn unto
The sultan's brothers, or his sons, delivers
His deadly anger; and, all hopes laid by,
Commands them to prepare themselves for heaven;
Which would stand with the quiet of your soul,
To think upon, and imitate.

DONUSA
Give me leave
A little to complain; first, of the hard
Condition of my fortune, which may move you,
Though not to rise up intercessors for me,
Yet, in remembrance of my former life,

(This being the first spot tainting mine honour,)
To be the means to bring me to his presence:
And then I doubt not, but I could allege
Such reasons in mine own defence, or plead
So humbly, (my tears helping,) that it should
Awake his sleeping pity.

ASAMBEG
'Tis in vain.
If you have aught to say, you shall have hearing;
And, in me, think him present.

DONUSA
I would thus then
First kneel, and kiss his feet; and after, tell him
How long I had been his darling; what delight
My infant years afforded him; how dear
He prized his sister in both bloods, my mother:
That she, like him, had frailty, that to me
Descends as an inheritance; then conjure him,
By her blest ashes, and his father's soul,
The sword that rides upon his thigh, his right hand
Holding the sceptre and the Othoman fortune,
To have compassion on me.

ASAMBEG
But suppose
(As I am sure) he would be deaf, what then
Could you infer?

DONUSA
I, then, would thus rise up,
And to his teeth tell him he was a tyrant,
A most voluptuous and insatiable epicure
In his own pleasures; which he hugs so dearly,
As proper and peculiar to himself,
That he denies a moderate lawful use
Of all delight to others. And to thee,
Unequal judge, I speak as much, and charge thee,
But with impartial eyes to look into
Thyself, and then consider with what justice
Thou canst pronounce my sentence. Unkind nature,
To make weak women servants, proud men masters!
Indulgent Mahomet, do thy bloody laws
Call my embraces with a Christian death,
Having my heat and May of youth, to plead
In my excuse? and yet want power to punish
These that, with scorn, break through thy cobweb edicts,

And laugh at thy decrees? To tame their lusts
There's no religious bit: let her be fair,
And pleasing to the eye, though Persian,
Moor,
Idolatress, Turk, or Christian, you are privileged,
And freely may enjoy her. At this instant,
I know, unjust man, thou hast in thy power
A lovely Christian virgin; thy offence
Equal, if not transcending mine: why, then,
(We being both guilty,) dost thou not descend
From that usurp'd tribunal, and with me
Walk hand in hand to death?

ASAMBEG
She raves; and we
Lose time to hear her: Read the law.

DONUSA
Do, do;
I stand resolved to suffer.

AGA [reads]
If any virgin, of what
degree, or quality soever, born a natural
Turk, shall be convicted of corporal looseness, and incontinence with, any Christian,
she is, by the decree of our great prophet,
Mahomet, to lose her head.

ASAMBEG
Mark that, then tax our justice!

AGA
Ever provided. That if she, the said offender, by any reasons, arguments, or persuasion, can win and
prevail with the said Christian offending with her, to alter his religion, and marry her, that then the
winning' of a soul to the Mahometan sect, shall acquit her from all shame, disgrace, and Punishment
whatsoever.

DONUSA
I lay hold on that clause, and challenge from you
The privilege of the law.

MUSTAPHA
What will you do?

DONUSA
Grant me access and means, I'll undertake
To turn this Christian Turk, and marry him:

This trial you cannot deny.

MUSTAPHA
Obase!
Can fear to die make you descend so low
From your high birth, and brand the Othoman line
With such a mark of infamy?

ASAMBEG
This is worse
Than the parting with your honour. Better suffer
Ten thousand deaths, and without hope to have
A place in our great prophet's paradise,
Than have an act to aftertimes remember'd,
So foul as this is.

MUSTAPHA
Cheer your spirits, madam;
To die is nothing, 'tis but parting with
A mountain of vexations.

ASAMBEG
Think of your honour:
In dying nobly, you make satisfaction
For your offence, and you shall live a story
Of bold heroic courage.

DONUSA
You shall not fool me
Out of my life: I claim the law, and sue for
A speedy trial; if I fail, you may
Determine of me as you please.

ASAMBEG
Base woman!
But use thy ways, and see thou prosper in them;
For, if thou fall again into my power,
Thou shalt in vain, after a thousand tortures,
Cry out for death, that death which now thou fliest from.
Unloose the prisoner's chains. Go, lead her on,
To try the magic of her tongue. I follow:

[Exeunt all but **ASAMBEG**.

I'm on the rack descend, my best Paulina.

[Exit with **PAULINA**.

SCENE III. A Room in the Prison

Enter **FRANCISCO** and **GAOLER**.

FRANCISCO
I come not empty-handed; I will purchase
Your favour at what rate you please. There's gold.

GAOLER
'Tis the best oratory. I will hazard
A check for your content. Below, there!

VITELLI [below]
Welcome!
Art thou the happy messenger, that brings me
News of my death?

GAOLER
Your hand.

[Plucks up **VITELLI**.

FRANCISCO
Now, if you please,
A little privacy.

GAOLER
You have bought it, sir;
Enjoy it freely.

[Exit.

FRANCISCO
O, my dearest pupil!
Witness these tears of joy, I never saw you,
Till now, look lovely; nor durst I ever glory
In the mind of any man I had built up
With the hands of virtuous and religious precepts,
Till this glad minute. Now you have made good
My expectation of you. By my order,
All Roman Caesars, that led kings in chains,
Fast bound to their triumphant chariots, if
Compared with that true glory and full lustre
You now appear in; all their boasted honours,
Purchased with blood and wrong, would lose their names,
And be no more remember'd!

VITELLI

This applause,
Confirm'd in your allowance, joys me more
Than if a thousand full-cramm'd theatres
Should clap their eager hands, to witness that
The scene I act did please, and they admire it.
But these are, father, but beginnings, not
The ends, of my high aims. I grant, to have master'd
The rebel appetite of flesh and blood,
Was far above my strength; and still owe for it
To that great Power that lent it: but, when I
Shall make't apparent the grim looks of Death
Affright me not, and that I can put off
The fond desire of life, (that, like a garment,
Covers and clothes our frailty,) hastening to
My martyrdom, as to a heavenly banquet,
To which I was a choice invited guest;
Then you may boldly say, you did not plough,
Or trust the barren and ungrateful sands
With the fruitful grain of your religious counsels.

FRANCISCO

You do instruct your teacher. Let the sun
Of your clear life, that lends to good men light,
But set as gloriously as it did rise,
(Though sometimes clouded,) you may write nil ultra
To human wishes.

VITELLI

I have almost gain'd
The end o' the race, and will not faint or tire now.

[Re-enter **GAOLER** with **AGA**.

AGA

Sir, by your leave, nay, stay not,

[To the **GAOLER**, who goes out]

I bring comfort.
The viceroy, taken with the constant bearing
Of your afflictions; and presuming too
You will not change your temper, does command
Your irons should be ta'en off.

[They take off his irons.

Now arm yourself
With your old resolution; suddenly
You shall be visited. You must leave the room too,
And do it without reply.

FRANCISCO
There's no contending:
Be still thyself, my son.

[Exeunt **AGA** and **FRANCISCO**.

VITELLI
'Tis not in man

[Enter **DONUSA**, followed at a distance by **ASAMBEG**, **MUSTAPHA**, and **PAULINA**.

To change or alter me.

PAULINA
Whom do I look on?
My brother? 'tis he! but no more, my tongue;
Thou wilt betray all. [Aside.

ASAMBEG
Let us hear this temptress:
The fellow looks as he would stop his ears
Against her powerful spells.

PAULINA
He is undone else. [Aside.

VITELLI
I'll stand the encounter charge me home.

DONUSA
I come, sir,

[Bows herself.

A beggar to you, and doubt not to find
A good man's charity, which if you deny,
You are cruel to yourself; a crime a wise man
(And such I hold you) would not willingly
Be guilty of: nor let it find less welcome,
Though I, a creature you contemn, now shew you
The way to certain happiness; nor think it
Imaginary or fantastical,
And so not worth the acquiring, in respect

The passage to it is nor rough nor thorny;
No steep hills in the way which you must climb up,
No monsters to be conquer'd, no enchantments
To be dissolved by counter charms, before
You take possession of it.

VITELLI
What strong poison
Is wrapp'd up in these sugar'd pills?

DONUSA
My suit is,
That you would quit your shoulders of a burthen,
Under whose ponderous weight you wilfully
Have too long groan'd, to cast those fetters off,
With which, with your own hands, you chain your freedom:
Forsake a severe, nay, imperious mistress,
Whose service does exact perpetual cares,
Watchings, and troubles; and give entertainment
To one that courts you, whose least favours are
Variety, and choice of all delights
Mankind is capable of.

VITELLI
You speak in riddles.
What burthen, or what mistress, or what fetters,
Are those you point at?

DONUSA
Those which your religion,
The mistress you too long have served, compels you
To bear with slave-like patience.

VITELLI
Ha!

PAULINA
How bravely
That virtuous anger shews?

DONUSA
Be wise, and weigh
The prosperous success of things; if blessings
Are donatives from heaven, (which, you must grant,
Were blasphemy to question,) and that
They are call'd down and pour'd on such as are
Most gracious with the great Disposer of them,
Look on our flourishing empire, if the splendor,

The majesty, and glory of it dim not
Your feeble sight; and then turn back, and see
The narrow bounds of yours, yet that poor remnant
Rent in as many factions and opinions
As you have petty kingdoms; and then, if
You are not obstinate against truth and reason,
You must confess the Deity you worship
Wants care or power to help you.

PAULINA
Hold out now,
And then thou art victorious. [Aside.

ASAMBEG
How he eyes her!

MUSTAPHA
As if he would look through her.

ASAMBEG
His eyes flame too,
As threatening violence.

VITELLI
But that I know
The devil, thy tutor, fills each part about thee,
And that I cannot play the exorcist
To dispossess thee, unless I should tear
Thy body limb by limb, and throw it to
The Furies, that expect it; I would now
Pluck out that wicked tongue, that hath blasphemed
The great Omnipotency, at whose nod
The fabric of the world shakes. Dare you bring
Your juggling prophet in comparison with
That most inscrutable and infinite Essence,
That made this All, and comprehends his work!
The place is too profane to mention him
Whose only name is sacred. O Donusa!
How much, in my compassion, I suffer,
That thou, on whom this most excelling form,
And faculties of discourse, beyond a woman.
Were by his liberal gift conferr'd, shouldst still
Remain in ignorance of him that gave it!
I will not foul my mouth to speak the sorceries
Of your seducer, his base birth, his whoredoms,
His strange impostures; nor deliver how
He taught a pigeon to feed in his ear,
Then made his credulous followers believe

It was an angel, that instructed him
In the framing of his Alcoran pray you, mark me.

ASAMBEG
These words are death, were he in nought else guilty.

VITELLI
Your intent to win me.
To be of your belief, proceeded from
Your fear to die. Can there be strength in that
Religion, that suffers us to tremble
At that which every day, nay hour, we haste to?

DONUSA
This is unanswerable, and there's something tells me
I err in my opinion.

VITELLI
Cherish it,
It is a heavenly prompter; entertain
This holy motion, and wear on your forehead
The sacred badge he arms his servants with;
You shall, like me, with scorn look down upon
All engines tyranny can advance to batter
Your constant resolution. Then you shall
Look truly fair, when your mind's pureness answers
Your outward beauties.

DONUSA
I came here to take you,
But I perceive a yielding in myself
To be your prisoner.

VITELLI
'Tis an overthrow,
That will outshine all victories. O Donusa,
Die in my faith, like me; and 'tis a marriage
At which celestial angels shall be waiters,
And such as have been sainted welcome us:
Are you confirm 'd?

DONUSA
I would be; but the means
That may assure me?

VITELLI
Heaven is merciful,
And will not suffer you to want a man

To do that sacred office, build upon it.

DONUSA
Then thus I spit at Mahomet.

ASAMBEG [coming forward]
Stop her mouth:
In death to turn apostata! I'll not hear
One syllable from any. Wretched creature!
With the next rising sun prepare to die.
Yet, Christian, in reward of thy brave courage,
Be thy faith right or wrong, receive this favour;
In person I'll attend thee to thy death:
And boldly challenge all that I can give,
But what's not in my grant, which is to
live.

[Exeunt.

ACT V

SCENE I. A Room in the Prison

Enter **VITELLI** and **FRANCISCO**.

FRANCISCO
You are wondrous brave and jocund.

VITELLI
Welcome, father.
Should I spare cost, or not wear cheerful looks
Upon my wedding day, it were ominous,
And shew'd I did repent it; which I dare not,
It being a marriage, howsoever sad
In the first ceremonies that confirm it,
That will for ever arm me against fears,
Repentance, doubts, or jealousies, and bring
Perpetual comforts, peace of mind, and quiet
To the glad couple.

FRANCISCO
I well understand you;
And my full joy to see you so resolved
Weak words cannot express. What is the hour
Design'd for this solemnity?

VITELLI

The sixth:
Something before the setting of the sun,
We take our last leave of his fading light,
And with our soul's eyes seek for beams eternal.
Yet there's one scruple with which I am much
Perplex'd and troubled, which I know you can
Resolve me of.

FRANCISCO

Whatis't?

VITELLI

This, sir; my bride,
Whom I first courted, and then won, not with
Loose lays, poor flatteries, apish compliments,
But sacred and religious zeal, yet wants
The holy badge that should proclaim her fit
For these celestial nuptials: willing she is,
I know, to wear it, as the choicest jewel,
On her fair forehead; but to you, that well
Could do that work of grace, I know the viceroy
Will never grant access. Now, in a case
Of this necessity, I would gladly learn,
Whether, in me, a layman, without orders,
It may not be religious and lawful,
As we go to our deaths, to do that office?

FRANCISCO

A question in itself with much ease answer'd:
Midwives, upon necessity, perform it;
And knights that, in the Holy Land, fought for
The freedom of Jerusalem, when full
Of sweat and enemies' blood, have made their helmets
The fount, out of which, with their holy hands.
They drew that heavenly liquor; 'twas approved then
By the holy church, nor must I think it now,
In you, a work less pious.

VITELLI

You confirm me;
I will find a way to do it. In the mean time,
Your holy vows assist me!

FRANCISCO

They shall ever
Be present with you.

VITELLI
You shall see me act
This last scene to the life.

FRANCISCO
And though now fall,
Rise a bless'd martyr.

VITELLI
That's my end, my all.

[Exeunt.

SCENE II. A Street

Enter **GRIMALDI**, **MASTER**, **BOATWAIN**, and **SAILORS**.

BOATSWAIN
Sir, if you slip this opportunity,
Never expect the like.

MASTER
With as much ease now
We may steal the ship out of the harbour, captain,
As ever gallants, in a wanton bravery,
Have set upon a drunken constable,
And bore him from a sleepy rug-gown'd watch:
Be therefore wise.

GRIMALDI
 I must be honest too.
And you shall wear that shape, you shall observe me,
If that you purpose to continue mine.
Think you ingratitude can be the parent
To our unfeign'd repentance? Do I owe
A peace within here, kingdoms could not purchase,
To my religious creditor, to leave him
Open to danger, the great benefit
Never remembered! no; though in her bottom
We could stow up the tribute of the Turk;
Nay, grant the passage safe too; I will never
Consent to weigh an anchor up, till he,
That only must, commands it.

BOATSWAIN
This religion

Will keep us slaves and beggars.

MASTER
The fiend prompts me
To change my copy: plague upon't! we are seamen;
What have we to do with't, but for a snatch or so,
At the end of a long Lent?

[Enter **FRANCISCO**.

BOATSWAIN
Mum: see who is here.

GRIMALDI
My father!

FRANCISCO
My good convert. I am full
Of serious business which denies me leave
To hold long conference with you: only thus much
Briefly receive; a day or two, at the most,
Shall make me fit to take my leave of Tunis,
Or give me lost for ever.

GRIMALDI
Days nor years,
Provided that my stay may do you service,
But to me shall be minutes.

FRANCISCO
I much thank you:
In this small scroll you may in private read
What my intents are; and, as they grow ripe,
I will instruct you further: in the mean time
Borrow your late distracted looks and gesture;
The more dejected you appear, the less
The viceroy must suspect you.

GRIMALDI
I am nothing,
But what you please to have me be.

FRANCISCO
Farewell, sir.
Be cheerful, master, something we will do,
That shall reward itself in the performance;
And that's true prize indeed.

MASTER
I am obedient.

BOATSWAIN
And I: there's no contending.

[Exeunt **GRIMALDI**, **MASTER**, **BOATSWAIN** and **SAILORS**.

FRANCISCO
Peace to you all!
Prosper, thou Great Existence, my endeavours,
As they religiously are undertaken,
And distant equally from servile gain,

[Enter **PAULINA**, **CARAZIE**, and **MANTO**.

Or glorious ostentation! I am heard,
In this blest opportunity, which in vain
I long have waited for. I must show myself.
O, she has found me! now if she prove right,
All hope will not forsake us.

PAULINA
Further off;
And in that distance know your duties too.
You were bestow'd on me as slaves to serve me,
And not as spies to pry into my actions,
And after, to betray me. You shall find
If any look of mine be unobserved,
I am not ignorant of a mistress' power,
And from whom I receive it.

CARAZIE
Note this, Manto,
The pride and scorn with which she entertains us,
Now we are made hers by the viceroy's gift!
Our sweet condition'd princess, lair Donusa,
Rest in her death wait on her? never used us
With such contempt. I would he had sent me
To the gallies, or the gallows, when he gave me
To this proud little devil.

MANTO
I expect
All tyrannous usage, but I must be patient;
And though, ten times a day, she tears these locks,
Or makes this face her footstool, 'tis but justice.

PAULINA

'Tis a true story of my fortunes, father.
My chastity preserved by miracle,
Or your devotions for me; and, believe it,
What outward pride soe'er I counterfeit,
Or state, to these appointed to attend me,
I am not in my disposition alter'd,
But still your humble daughter, and share with you
In my poor brother's sufferings: all hell's torments
Revenge it on accurs'd Grimaldi's soul,
That, in his rape of me, gave a beginning
To all the miseries that since have follow'd I

FRANCISCO

Be charitable, and forgive him, gentle daughter.
He's a changed man, and may redeem his fault
In his fair life hereafter. You must bear too
Your forced captivity, for 'tis no better,
Though you wear golden fetters, and of him,
Whom death affrights not, learn to hold out nobly.

PAULINA

You are still the same good counsellor.

FRANCISCO

And who knows,
(Since what above is purposed, is inscrutable,)
But that the viceroys's extreme dotage on you
May be the parent of a happier birth
Than yet our hopes dare fashion. Longer conference
May prove unsafe for you and me; however
(Perhaps for trial) he allows you freedom.

[Delivers a paper.

From this learn therefore what you must attempt,
Though with the hazard of yourself: heaven guard you,
And give Vitelli patience! then I doubt not
But he will have a glorious uay, since some
Hold truly, such as suffer, overcome.

[Exeunt.

SCENE III. A Hall in Asambeg's Palace

Enter **ASAMBEG, MUSTAPHA, AGA**, and **CAPIAGA**.

ASAMBEG

What we commanded, see perform 'd; and fail not
In all things to be punctual.

AGA

We shall, sir.

[Exeunt **AGA** and **CAPIAGA**.

MUSTAPHA

Tis strange, that you should use such circumstance
To a delinquent of so mean condition.

ASAMBEG

Had he appeared in a more sordid shape
Than disguised greatness ever deign'd to mask in,
The gallant bearing of his present fortune
Aloud proclaims him noble.

MUSTAPHA

If you doubt him
To be a man built up for great employments,
And, as a cunning spy, sent to explore
The city's strength or weakness, you by torture
May force him to discover it.

ASAMBEG

That were base;
Nor dare I do such injury to virtue
And bold assured courage; neither can I
Be won to think, but if I should attempt it,
I shoot against the moon. He that hath stood
The roughest battery, that captivity
Could ever bring to shake a constant temper;
Despised the fawnings of a future greatness,
By beauty, in her full perfection, tender'd;
That hears of death as of a quiet slumber,
And from the surplusage of his own firmness,
Can spare enough of fortitude, to assure
A feeble woman; will not, Mustapha,
Be alter'd in his soul for any torments
We can afflict his body with.

MUSTAPHA

Do your pleasure:
I only offer'd you a friend's advice,
But without gall or envy to the man

That is to suffer. But what do you determine
Of poor Grimaldi? the disgrace call'd on him,
I hear, has run him mad.

ASAMBEG
There weigh the difference
In the true temper of their minds. The one,
A pirate, sold to mischiefs, rapes, and all
That make a slave relentless and obdurate,
Yet, of himself wanting the inward strengths
That should defend him, sinks beneath compassion
Or pity of a man: whereas this merchant,
Acquainted only with a civil life;
Arm'd in himself, intrench'd and fortified
With his own virtue, valuing life and death
At the same price, poorly does not invite
A favour, but commands us to do him right;
Which unto him, and her we both once honour'd
As a just debt, I gladly pay; they enter.
Now sit we equal hearers.

[A dreadful music.

[Enter at one door, the **AGA**, **JANIZARIES**, **VITELLI**, **FRANCISCO**, and **GAZET**; at the other, **DONUSA**, (her train borne-up, **PAULINA**, **CARAZIE**, and **MANTO**.

MUSTAPHA
I shall hear
And see, sir, without passion; my wrongs arm me.

VITELLI
A joyful preparation! To whose bounty
Owe we our thanks for gracing thus our hymen?
The notes, though dreadful to the ear, sound here
As our epithalamium were sung
By a celestial choir, and a full chorus
Assured us future happiness. These that lead me
Gaze not with wanton eyes upon my bride,
Nor for their service are repaid by me
With jealousies or fears; nor do they envy
My passage to those pleasures from which death
Cannot deter me. Great sir, pardon me:
Imagination of the joys I haste to
Made me forget my duty; but the form
And ceremony past, I will attend you,
And with our constant resolution feast you;
Not with coarse cates, forgot as soon as tasted,
But such as shall, while you have memory,

Be pleasing to the palate.

FRANCISCO
Be not lost
In what you purpose.

[Exit.

GAZET
Call you this a marriage!
It differs little from hanging; I cry at it.

VITELLI
See, where my bride appears! in what full lustre!
As if the virgins that bear up her train
Had long contended to receive an honour
Above their births, in doing her this service
Nor comes she fearful to meet those delights,
Which, once past o'er, immortal pleasures follow.
I need not, therefore, comfort or encourage
Her forward steps; and I should offer wrong
To her mind's fortitude, should I but ask
How she can brook the rough high-going sea,
Over whose foamy back our ship, well rigg'd
With hope and strong assurance, must transport us.
Nor will I tell her, when we reach the haven,
Which tempests shall not hinder, what loud welcome
Shall entertain us; nor commend the place,
To tell whose least perfection would strike dumb
The eloquence of all boasted in story,
Though join'd together.

DONUSA
'Tis enough, my dearest,
I dare not doubt you; as your humble shadow,
Lead where you please, I follow.

VITELLI
One suit, sir,
And willingly I cease to be a beggar;
And that you may with more security hear it,
Know, 'tis not life I'll ask, nor to defer.
Our deaths, but a few minutes.

ASAMBEG
Speak; 'tis granted.

VITELLI

We being now to take our latest leave,
And grown of one belief, I do desire
I may have your allowance to perform it,
But in the fashion which we Christians use
Upon the like occasions.

ASAMBEG
'Tis allow'd of.

VITELLI
My service: haste, Gazet, to the next spring,
And bring me of it.

GAZET
Would I could as well
Fetch you a pardon; I would not run but fly,
And be here in a moment.

[Exit.

MUSTAPHA
What's the mystery
Of this? discover it.

VITELLI
Great sir, I'll tell you.
Each country hath its own peculiar rites:
Some, when they are to die, drink store of wine,
Which, pour'd in liberally, does oft beget
A bastard valour, with which arm'd, they bear
The not-to-be declined charge of death
With less fear and astonishment: others take
Drugs to procure a heavy sleep, that so
They may insensibly receive the means
That casts them in an everlasting slumber;
Others

[Re-enter **GAZET**, with water,

O welcome!

ASAMBEG
Now the use of yours?

VITELLI
The clearness of this is a perfect sign
Of innocence: and as this washes off
Stains and pollutions from the things we wear;

Thrown thus upon the forehead, it hath power
To purge those spots that cleave upon the mind.

[Sprinkles it on her face.

If thankfully received.

ASAMBEG
'Tis a strange custom.

VITELLI
How do you entertain it, my
Donusa?
Feel you no alteration, no new motives,
No unexpected aids, that may confirm you
In that to which you were inclined before?

DONUSA
I am another woman; till this minute
I never lived, nor durst think how to die.
How long have I been blind! yet on the sudden,
By this blest means, I feel the films of error
I Ta'en from my soul's eyes. O divine physician!
That hast bestow'd a sight on me, which
Death,
Though ready to embrace me in his arms,
Cannot take from me: let me kiss the hand
That did this miracle, and seal my thanks
Upon those lips from whence these sweet words vanish'd,
That freed me from the cruellest of prisons,
Blind ignorance and misbelief. False prophet!
Impostor Mahomet!

ASAMBEG
I'll hear no more,
You do abuse my favours; sever them:
Wretch, if thou hadst another life to lose,
This blasphemy deserved it; instantly
Carry them to their deaths.

VITELLI
We part now, blest one,
To meet hereafter in a kingdom, where
Hell's malice shall not reach us.

PAULINA
Ha! ha! ha!

ASAMBEG
What means my mistress?

PAULINA
Who can hold her spleen,
When such ridiculous follies are presented,
The scene, too, made religion? O, my lord,
How from one cause two contrary effects
Spring up upon the sudden!

ASAMBEG
This is strange.

PAULINA
That which hath fool'd her in her death, wins me,
That hitherto have barr'd myself from pleasure,
To live in all delight.

ASAMBEG
There's music in this.

PAULINA
I now will run as fiercely to your arms
As ever longing woman did, borne high
On the swift wings of appetite.

VITELLI
O devil!

PAULINA
Nay, more; for there shall be no odds betwixt us,
I will turn Turk.

GAZET
Most of your tribe do so,
When they begin in whore. [Aside.

ASAMBEG
You are serious, lady?

PAULINA
Serious! but satisfy me in a suit
That to the world may witness that I have
Some power upon you, and to-morrow challenge
Whatever's in my gift; for I will be
At your dispose.

GAZET

That's ever the subscription
To a damn'd whore's false epistle. [Aside.

ASAMBEG
Ask this hand,
Or, if thou wilt, the heads of these. I am rapt
Beyond myself with joy. Speak, speak, what is it?

PAULINA
But twelve short hours' reprieve for this base couple.

ASAMBEG
The reason, since you hate them?

PAULINA
That I may
Have time to triumph o'er this wretched woman.
I'll be myself her guardian; I will feast,
Adorned in her choice and richest jewels:
Commit him to what guards you please.
Grant this,
I am no more mine own, but yours.

ASAMBEG
Enjoy it;
Repine at it who dares: bear him safe off
To the black tower, but give him all things useful:
The contrary was not in your request?

PAULINA
I do contemn him.

DONUSA
Peace in death denied me!

PAULINA
Thou shalt not go in liberty to thy grave;
For one night a sultana is my slave.

MUSTAPHA
A terrible little tyranness!

ASAMBEG
No more;
Her will shall be a law. Till now ne'er happy!

[Exeunt.

Enter **FRANCISCO, GRIMALDI, MASTER, BOATSWAIN,** and **SAILORS**.

GRIMALDI
Sir, all things are in readiness; the Turks,
That seized upon my ship, stow'd under hatches;
My men resolved and cheerful. Use but means
To get out of the ports, we will be ready
To bring you aboard, and then (heaven be but pleased)
This, for the viceroy's fleet!

FRANCISCO
Discharge your parts;
In mine I'll not be wanting: Fear not, master;
Something will come along to fraught your bark,
That you will have just cause to say you never
Made such a voyage.

MASTER
We will stand the hazard.

FRANCISCO
What's the best hour?

BOATSWAIN
After the second watch.

FRANCISCO
Enough; each to his charge.

GRIMALDI
We will be careful.

[Exeunt.

Enter **PAULINA, DONUSA, CARAZIE,** and **MANTO**.

PAULINA
Sit, madam, it is fit that I attend you;
And pardon, I beseech you, my rude language,
To which the sooner you will be invited,

When you shall understand, no way was left me
To free you from a present execution,
But by my personating that which never
My nature was acquainted with.

DONUSA
I believe you.

PAULINA
You will, when you shall understand I may
Receive the honour to be known unto you
By a nearer name: and, not to rack you further,
The man you please to favour is my brother;
No merchant, madam, but a gentleman
Of the best rank in Venice.

DONUSA
I rejoice in't;
But what's this to his freedom? for myself,
Were he well off, I were secure.

PAULINA
I have
A present means, not plotted by myself,
But a religious man, my confessor,
That may preserve all, if we had a servant
Whose faith we might rely on.

DONUSA
She, that's now
Your slave, was once mine; had I twenty lives,
I durst commit them to her trust.

MANTO
O madam!
I have been false, forgive me: I'll redeem it
By anything, however desperate,
You please to impose upon me.

PAULINA
Troth, these tears,
I think, cannot be counterfeit; I believe her,
And, if you please, will try her.

DONUSA
At your peril;
There is no further danger can look towards me.

PAULINA
This only then canst thou use means to carry
This bake-meat to Vitelli?

MANTO
With much ease;
I am familiar with the guard; beside,
It being known it was I that betray'd him,
My entrance hardly will of them be question'd.

PAULINA
About it then. Say, that 'twas sent to him
From his Donusa; bid him search the midst of it,
He there shall find a cordial.

MANTO
What I do
Shall speak my care and faith.

[Exit.

DONUSA
Good fortune with thee!

PAULINA
You cannot eat?

DONUSA
The time we thus abuse
We might employ much better.

PAULINA
I am glad
To hear this from you. As for you, Carazie,
If our intents do prosper, make choice, whether
You'll steal away with your two mistresses,
Or take your fortune.

CARAZIE
I'll be gelded twice first;
Hang him that stays behind.

PAULINA
 I wait you, madam.
Were but my brother off, by the command
Of the doting viceroy there's no guard dare stay me;
And I will safely bring you to the place,
Where we must expect him.

DONUSA
Heaven be gracious to us!

[Exeunt.

SCENE VI. A Room in the Black Tower

Enter **VITELLI**, **AGA**, and **GUARD**, at the door.

VITELLI
Paulina to fall off thus! 'tis to me
More terrible than death, and, like an earthquake,
Totters this walking building, such I am;
And in my sudden ruin would prevent,
By choaking up at once my vital spirits,
This pompous preparation for my death.
But I am lost; that good man, good Francisco,
Deliver'd me a paper, which till now
I wanted leisure to peruse.

[Reads the paper.

AGA
This Christian
Fears not, it seems, the near approaching sun,
Whose second rise he never must salute.

[Enter **MANTO** with the baked-meat.

1ST GUARD
Who's that?

2ND GUARD
Stand.

AGA
Manto!

MANTO
Here's the viceroy's ring,
Gives warrant to my entrance; yet you may
Partake of anything I shall deliver.
'Tis but a present to a dying man,
Sent from the princess that must suffer with him.

AGA
Use your own freedom.

MANTO
I would not disturb
This his last contemplation.

VITELLI
O, 'tis well!
He has restored all, and I at peace again
With my Paulina.

MANTO
Sir, the sad Donusa,
Grieved for your sufferings, more than for her own,
Knowing the long and tedious pilgrimage
You are to take, presents you with this cordial,
Which privately she wishes you should taste of;
And search the middle part, where you shall find
Something that hath the operation to
Make death look lovely.

VITELLI
I will not dispute
What she commands, but serve it.

[Exit.

AGA
Prithee, Manto,
How hath the unfortunate princess spent this night,
Under her proud new mistress?

MANTO
With such patience
As it o'ercomes the other's insolence,
Nay, triumphs o'er her pride. My much: haste now
Commands me hence; but, the sad tragedy past,
I'll give you satisfaction to the full
Of all hath pass'd, and a true character
Of the proud Christian's nature.

[Exit,

AGA
Break the watch up;
What should we fear i' the midst of our own strengths?
'Tis but the basha's jealousy. Farewell, soldiers!

[Exeunt.

SCENE VII. An Upper Room in the Same

Enter **VITELLI** with the baked-meat.

VITELLI
There's something more in this than means to cloy
A hungry appetite, which I must discover.
She will'd me search the midst: thus, thus
I pierce it.
Ha! what is this? a scroll bound up in a packthread!
What may the mystery be?
[Reads.
Son, let down this packthread at the west window of the castle. By it you shall draw up a ladder of
ropes, by which you may descend: your dearest Donusa with the rest of your friends below attend you.
Heaven prosper you! best of men! he that gives up himself
To a true religious friend, leans not upon
A false deceiving reed, but boldly builds
Upon a rock; which now with joy I find
In reverend Francisco, whose good vows,
Labours, and watchings, in my hoped-for freedom,
Appear a pious miracle. I come,
I come with confidence; though the descent
Were steep as hell, I know I cannot slide,
Being call'd dpwn by such a faithful guide.

[Exit.

SCENE VIII. A Room in Asambeg's Palace

Enter **ASAMBEG, MUSTAPHA**, and **JANIZARIES**.

ASAMBEG
Excuse me, Mustapha, though this night to me
Appear as tedious as that treble one
Was to the world, when Jove on fair Alcmena
Begot Alcides. Were you to encounter
Those ravishing pleasures, which the slow paced hours
(To me they are such) bar me from, you would,
With your continued wishes, strive to imp
New feathers to the broken wings of time,
And chide the amorous sun, for too long dalliance

In Thetis' watery bosom.

MUSTAPHA
You are too violent
In your desires, of which you are yet uncertain;
Having no more assurance to enjoy them,
Than a weak woman's promise, on which wise men
Faintly rely.

ASAMBEG
Tush! she is made of truth;
And what she says she will do, holds as firm
As laws in brass, that know no change:

[A chamber shot off.

What's this?
Some new prize brought in, sure

[Enter **AGA** hastily.

Why are thy looks
So ghastly? Villain, speak!

AGA
Great sir, hear me,
Then after, kill me: we are all betray f d.
The false Grimaldi, sunk in your disgrace,
With his confederates, has seized his ship,
And those that guarded it stowed under hatches.
With him the condemn'd princess, and the merchant,
That, with a ladder made of ropes, descended
From the black tower, in which he was enclosed,
And your fair mistress

ASAMBEG
Ha!

AGA
With all their train,
And choicest jewels, are gone safe aboard:
Their sails spread forth, and with a fore right gale
Leaving our coast, in scorn of all pursuit,
As a farewell, they shew'd a broadside to us.

ASAMBEG
No more.

MUSTAPHA
Now note your confidence!

ASAMBEG
No more.
O my credulity! I am too full
Of grief and rage to speak. Dull, heavy fool!
Worthy of all the tortures that the frown
Of thy incensed master can throw on thee,
Without one man's compassion! I will hide
This head among the desarts, or some cave
Fill'd with my shame and me; where I alone
May die without a partner in my moan.

[Exeunt.

PHILIP MASSINGER – A SHORT BIOGRAPHY

This biography was initially written in 1830

Very few materials exist for a life of Massinger beyond the entries of the Parish Register or the College Books, and a few slender intimations scattered here and there in the dedications to his plays. From these scanty sources the following brief memoir is derived.

Our author was born at Salisbury in the year 1584: he was the son of Arthur Massinger, a gentleman in the service of Henry, the second Earl of Pembroke. We must not suppose, from his being thus attached to the family of a nobleman, that the father of our poet was a person of inferior birth and station. In those days the word servant carried with it no sense of degradation. The great lords and officers of the court numbered inferior nobles among their followers. We read, in Cavendish's Life of Wolsey, that "my Lord Percy, the son and heir of the Earl of Northumberland, attended upon and was servitor to the lord-cardinal:" and from the situation which Arthur Massinger held in the household of so high and influential a person as the Earl of Pembroke, we might be justly led to argue rather favourably than unfavourably of his family and his connexions. "There were," says Mr. Gifford, "many considerations which united to render this state of dependance respectable and even honourable. The secretaries, clerks, and assistants, of various departments, were not then, as now, nominated by the government, but left to the choice of the person who held the employment; and as no particular dwelling was officially set apart for their residence, they were entertained in the house of their principal. That communication, too, between noblemen of power and trust, both of a public and private nature, which is now committed to the post, was in those days managed by confidential servants, who were despatched from one to the other, and even to the sovereign;" and, indeed, the father of our poet himself was, we know, in one instance thus employed as the bearer of communications from his patron to Elizabeth. We read in The Sidney Letters, "Mr. Massinger is newly come up from the Earl of Pembroke with letters to the queen for his lordship's leave to be away this St. George's Day." This was an errand which would not have been intrusted to the execution of any inconsiderable person: unimportant as the occasion may appear to us, it would not have been regarded in that light by Elizabeth; for no monarch ever exacted from the nobility, and particularly from her officers of state, a more rigid and scrupulous compliance with stated order than this princess.

With regard to the early youth of Massinger, we possess no information whatever. Mr. Gifford supposes that it might have been passed at Wilton, a seat belonging to the Earl of Pembroke, in the neighbourhood of Salisbury; but this mode of disposing of his early years rests on a very improbable conjecture. It may occasionally have happened that the child of a favourite dependant was admitted as the companion of the younger branches of the patron's family, and allowed to receive his education among them; but this was certainly not an ordinary case; and, like Cavendish, a large majority of the great man's servants and dependants "left wife and children, home and family, rest and quietness, only to serve him."—Massinger was most likely educated at the grammar-school of Salisbury, where many distinguished characters have received the rudiments of their education, among whom the elegant and accomplished Addison is to be numbered. But wherever the first years of our poet's life may have been spent, and whatever may have been the nature of his education, we know that at the age of eighteen (May 14, 1602) he was entered at the university of Oxford, and became a commoner of St. Alban's Hall.

Massinger resided at Oxford about four years, and then abruptly left it, without taking any degree. The cause of this sudden departure is ascribed by Mr. Gifford to the death of his father, from whom his supplies were derived: but Davies relates a very different story, and asserts that the Earl of Pembroke, who had sent him to the university and maintained him there, withdrew the necessary allowance in consequence of his having misapplied the time demanded for severer studies, in the pursuit of a more attractive but less profitable description of literature. Each opinion is equally ungrounded on the basis of any substantial evidence, and rests almost entirely on the imagination of the biographer: what slight authority there is favours the latter supposition, which, perhaps, on the whole, is most consistent with the known circumstances of the case. Anthony Wood, who was born, lived, and died at Oxford; who spent his time in collecting and recording the gossip which circulated in the university respecting the characters and conduct of its more distinguished sons; and whose evidence, however indifferent it may be, is the best that can be obtained upon the subject, confirms the representation of Davies:—"Massinger," says Wood, "gave his mind more to poetry and romance, for about four years or more, than to logic and philosophy, which he ought to have done, as he was patronised to that end." This passage corroborates the account of Davies so far as to intimate that patronage was afforded to our author, and that cause of dissatisfaction was given to the patron; but it goes no farther: it does not even state to whom the poet was indebted for assistance, nor that the misapplication of his academic hours was at all resented by the friend from whom the assistance was received: but still Wood is very probably correct in his information that other than his paternal funds were depended upon for maintaining Massinger at the university; and if such was the case, there can be no question from whose hands they must have proceeded; while the simple fact of his having been totally neglected, from the time of his father's death, by the whole of the Pembroke family, till after the demise of the earl, carries with it a strong suspicion that some offence was committed on the side of the poet, and tenaciously remembered on the side of the peer. Henry, the second Earl of Pembroke, died (1601) the year before Massinger was admitted at Oxford; and William, the third earl, to whom the father of Massinger continued attached during life, is universally and justly considered one of the brightest ornaments of the courts of Elizabeth and James. He was a man of generous and liberal disposition; the distinguished patron of arts and learning; and a lover of poetry, which he himself cultivated with some degree of success. It is not probable—it is impossible—that such a man should have allowed the highly talented son of an old and faithful servant of his family to be checked in his course of study, and abandoned to maintain, through the early years of life, a single-handed contest with adversity, for the want of that pecuniary aid which he could have yielded and never missed, unless some strong and decided cause of displeasure had existed. Had Massinger been merely forced to leave the university, as Mr. Gifford supposes, because the funds necessary to maintain him there had failed with the life of his father, we impute an act of illiberality to the Earl of Pembroke which is inconsistent with the whole tenor of his life and character. From whatever source the expenses of our author's education were originally defrayed, their suddenly ceasing argues in favour of the account intimated by Wood and detailed by Davies. If his father had, during his life, supported him at the university, there must have been some reason for the earl's not continuing that support when the father of Massinger was no more; and perhaps the most honourable supposition for both parties is that which represents the earl as offended by the bent of our author's studies and pursuits. By adopting this view of the case we are saved from the painful necessity of either assuming, on the one hand, that a nobleman distinguished among the most amiable characters of his age allowed a highly gifted and meritorious young man, a natural dependant of his house, to languish in the want of that countenance and protection on which he had an hereditary claim; or, on the other hand, that Massinger had incurred the displeasure of his natural and hereditary patron by the commission of some more crying offence.

Every, even the slightest, surmise of Mr. Gifford is deserving attention and respect; but I cannot admit the supposition by which he would account for the alienation that subsisted between the Earl of Pembroke and our author. That distinguished critic has inferred, from the religious sentiments contained in The Virgin Martyr, that Massinger was a Roman catholic, and for that cause neglected by the protector of his father. But if the intimations scattered through this play and others should be received as sufficient evidence of the faith of Massinger, we must, on similar evidence—the intimations contained in Measure for Measure, for instance—conclude that the religion of Shakspeare was the same; and then we are cast back upon our old difficulty, and have to explain why William Earl of Pembroke, a celebrated patron of literary men, and of dramatists in particular, scorned to yield his notice to the catholic Massinger, while (to use the expression of Heminge and Condell) he "prosequuted" the catholic Shakspeare and "his works with so much favour?" There are many reasons for believing Shakspeare to have been a member of the church of Rome; and the patronage afforded him by the Earl of Pembroke proves, that that nobleman extended his liberality to men of genius without any regard to distinctions of faith; but, on the other hand, we have no just grounds for assuming that Massinger really did hold the same opinions. The only evidence we have upon this point, that afforded by the general tone of his writings, is of a most vague and superficial description. What, in fact, can be inferred from it? We may from such a source derive very satisfactory information respecting the sentiments which would be favourably received by the audience, but very little respecting those of the author. The truth is, that though the national religion was reformed in its liturgy and articles, the feelings, prejudices, and superstitions of the people were still almost entirely catholic; and Massinger, like any other dramatic author, writing for the amusement of the people, necessarily addressed them in a language they would understand, and with sentiments that accorded with their own. Besides, as a poet, he would never carry his theological distinctions to his literary labours: Voltaire himself is catholic in his tragedies; and Massinger naturally adopted the creed which was most suitable to the purposes of poetry, and afforded the most picturesque ceremonies and romantic situations. I feel inclined, therefore, to dismiss entirely the theory suggested by Mr. Gifford, for these two reasons; first, supposing our author to have been a catholic, we have no reason for condemning the Earl of Pembroke as a bigot and a persecutor, who would close his eyes to the merits of so great an author, because his faith did not tally with his own; and, secondly, we have no sufficient grounds for supposing him to have been a catholic at all. But with regard to all such visionary conjectures, thinking is literally a waste of thought.

Whatever may have been the nature of Massinger's studies at Oxford, it is quite certain, from the general character of his works, that his time could not have been wasted there; and his literary acquirements, at the period of his leaving the university, appear to have been multifarious and extensive. He was about two-and-twenty (1606) when he arrived in London, where, as he more than once observes, he was driven by his necessities, and somewhat inclined, perhaps, by the peculiar bent of his talents, to dedicate himself to the service of the stage.

The theatre, when Massinger first took up his abode in the metropolis, must have presented attractions of all others the most calculated to excite the interest, and inspire the imagination, of a young man of sensibility, taste, and education like our poet. No art ever attained a more rapid maturity than the dramatic art in England. The people had, indeed, been long accustomed to a species of exhibition, called MIRACLES or MYSTERIES, founded on sacred subjects, and performed by the ministers of religion themselves, on the holy festivals, in or near the churches, and designed to instruct the ignorant in the leading facts of sacred history. From the occasional introduction of allegorical characters, such as Faith, Death, Hope, or Sin, into these religious dramas, representations of another kind, called MORALITIES, had by degrees arisen, of which the plots were more artificial, regular, and connected, and which were entirely formed of such personifications: but the first rough draught of a regular tragedy and comedy—Lord Sackville's Gorboduc, and Still's Gammer Gurton's Needle—were not produced till within the latter half of the sixteenth century, and little more than twenty years before the stage acquired its highest splendour in the productions of Shakspeare.

About the end of the sixteenth century, the attention of the public began to be more generally directed to the drama; and it throve most admirably beneath the cheering beams of popular favour. The theatrical performances which in the early part of Elizabeth's reign had been exhibited on temporary stages, erected in such halls or apartments as the actors could procure, or, more generally, in the yards of the larger inns, while the spectators surveyed them from the surrounding windows and galleries, began to find more convenient and permanent habitations. About the year 1569, a regular playhouse, under the appropriate name of The Theatre, was erected. It is supposed to have stood somewhere in Blackfriars; and, three years after the commencement of this establishment, the queen, yielding to her own inclination for such amusements, and disregarding the remonstrances of the Puritans, granted licence and authority to the servants of the Earl of Leicester ("for the recreation of her loving subjects, as for her own solace and pleasure when she should think good to see them") to exercise their occupation throughout the whole realm of England. From this time the number of theatres increased with the increasing demands of the people. Various noblemen had their respective companies of performers, who were associated as their servants, and acted under their protection; and when Massinger left Oxford, and commenced dramatic author, there were no less than seven principal theatres open in the metropolis.

With respect to the interior arrangements, there were very few points of difference between our modern theatres and those of the days of Massinger. The prices of admission, indeed, were considerably cheaper: to the boxes the entrance was a shilling; to the pit and galleries only sixpence. Sixpence also was the price paid for stools upon the stage; and these seats, as we learn from Decker's Gull's Hornbook, were particularly affected by the wits and critics of the time. The conduct of the audience was less restrained by the sense of public decorum, and smoking tobacco, playing at cards, eating and drinking, were generally prevalent among them. The hours of performance were also earlier: the play commencing at one o'clock. During the representation a flag was unfurled at the top of the theatre; and the stage, according to the universal practice of the age, was strewn with rushes; but, in all other respects, the theatres of Elizabeth and James's days seem to have borne a perfect resemblance to our own. They had their pit, where the inferior class of spectators, the groundlings, vented their clamorous censure or approbation; they had their boxes—rooms as they were called—to which the right of exclusive admission was engaged by the night, for the more affluent portion of the audience; and there were again the galleries, or scaffoldings above the boxes, for those who were content to purchase less commodious situations at a cheaper rate. On the stage, in the same manner, the appointments appear to have been nearly of the same description as at present. The curtain divided the audience from the actors, which, at the third sounding, not indeed of the bell, but of the trumpet, was drawn for the commencement of the performance. Malone, in his account of the ancient theatre, supposes that there were no moveable scenes; that a permanent elevation of about nine feet was raised at the back of the stage, from which, in many of the old plays, part of the dialogue was spoken; and that there was a private box on each side this platform. Such an arrangement would have destroyed all theatrical illusion; and it seems extraordinary that any spectators should desire to fix themselves in a station where they could have seen nothing but the backs and trains of the performers; but, as Malone himself acknowledges the spot to have been inconvenient, and that "it is not very easy to ascertain the precise situation where these boxes really were", it may very reasonably be presumed, that they were not placed in the position that the historian of the English stage has supposed. As to the permanent floor, or upper stage, of which he speaks, he may or may not be correct in his statement. All that his quotations upon the subject really establish is, that in the old, as in the modern theatre, when the actor was to speak from a window, or balcony, or the walls of a fortress, the requisite ingenuity was not wanting to contrive a representation of the place. But with regard to the use of painted moveable scenery, it is not possible, from the very circumstances of the case, to believe him correct in his theory. Such a contrivance could not have escaped our ancestors. All the materials were ready to their hands. They had not to invent for themselves, but merely to adapt an old invention to that peculiar purpose; and at a time when every better-furnished apartment was adorned with tapestry; when even the rooms of the commonest taverns were hung with painted cloths; while all the materials were constantly before their eyes, we can hardly believe our forefathers to have been so deficient in ingenuity, as to have missed the simple contrivance of converting the common ornaments of their walls into the decorations of their theatres. But, in fact, the use of scenery was almost co-existent with the introduction of dramatic representations in this country. In the Chester Mysteries (1268), the most ancient and complete collection of the kind which we possess, is found the following stage direction: "Then Noe shall go into the arke with all his familye, his wife excepte. The arke must be boarded round about; and upon the boardes all the beastes and fowles, hereafter rehearsed, must be painted, that their wordes may agree with their pictures." In this passage we have a clear reference to a painted scene. It is not likely that, in the lapse of three centuries, while all other arts were in a state of rapid improvement, and the art of dramatic writing, perhaps, more rapidly and successfully improved than any other, the art of theatrical decoration should have alone stood still. It is not improbable that their scenes were few; and that they were varied, as occasion might require, by the introduction of different pieces of stage furniture. Mr. Gifford, who adheres to the opinions of Malone, says, "A table with a pen and ink thrust in, signified that the stage was a counting-house; if these were withdrawn and two stools put in their place, it was then a tavern." And this might be perfectly satisfactory as long as the business of the play was supposed to be passing within doors; but when it was removed to the open air, such meagre devices would no longer be sufficient to guide the imagination of the audience, and some new method must have been adopted to indicate the place of action. After giving the subject very considerable attention, I cannot help thinking that Steevens was right in rejecting Malone's theory, and concluding that the spectators were, as at the present day, assisted in following the progress of the story by means of painted moveable scenery. This opinion is confirmed by the ancient stage directions. In the folio Shakspeare, 1623, we read "Enter Brutus in his orchard; Enter Timon in the woods; Enter Timon from the cave." In Coriolanus, "Marcius follows them to the gates and is shut in." Innumerable instances of the same kind might be cited to prove that the ancient stage was not so defective in the necessary decorations as some antiquaries of great authority would represent. "It may be added," says Steevens, "that the dialogue of our old dramatists has such perpetual reference to objects supposed visible to the audience, that the want of scenery could not have failed to render many of the descriptions absurd. Banquo examines the outside of Inverness castle with such minuteness, that he distinguishes even the nests which the martens had built under the projecting part of its roof. Romeo, standing in a garden, points to the tops of fruit-trees gilded by the moon. The prologue speaker to the second part of Henry the Fourth expressly shows the spectators 'This worm-eaten hold of ragged stone,' in which Northumberland was lodged. Iachimo takes the most exact inventory of every article in Imogen's bed-chamber, from the silk and silver of which her tapestry was wrought, down to the Cupids that support her andirons. Had not the inside of the apartment, with its proper furniture, been represented, how ridiculous must the action of Iachimo have appeared! He must have stood looking out of the room for the particulars supposed to be visible within it." The works of Massinger would afford innumerable instances of a similar kind to vindicate the opinion which Steevens has asserted on the testimony of Shakspeare alone. But on this subject there is one passage which appears to me quite conclusive. Must not all the humour of the mock play in The Midsummer Night's Dream have been entirely lost, unless the audience before whom it was performed were accustomed to all the embellishments requisite to give effect to a dramatic representation, and could consequently estimate the absurdity of those shallow contrivances and mean substitutes for scenery devised by the ignorance of the clowns?

In only one respect do I perceive any material difference between the mode of representation at the time of Massinger and at present: in his day, the female parts were performed by boys. This custom, which must in many cases have materially injured the illusion of the scene, was in others of considerable advantage: it furnished the stage with a succession of youths, regularly educated for the art, to fill, in every department of the drama, the characters suited to their age. When the lad had become too tall for Juliet, he had acquired the skill, and was most admirably fitted, both in age and appearance, for performing the part which Garrick considered the most difficult on the stage, because it needed "an old head upon young shoulders," the ardent and arduous character of Romeo. When the voice had "the mannish crack," that rendered the youth unfit to appear as the representative of the gentle Imogen, the stage possessed in him the very person that was wanting to do justice to the princely sentiments of Arviragus or Guiderius.

Such was the state of the stage when Massinger arrived in the metropolis, and dedicated his talents to its service. He joined a splendid fraternity, for Shakspeare, Jonson, Beaumont, Fletcher, Shirley, were then flourishing at the height of their reputation, and the full vigour of their genius. Massinger came among them no unworthy competitor for such honours and emoluments as the theatre could afford. Of the honours, indeed, he seems to have reaped a very fair and equitable portion; of the emoluments, the harvest was less abundant. In those days, very little pecuniary reward was to be gained by the dramatic poet, unless, as indeed was most frequently the case, he added the profession of the actor to that of the author, and recited the verses which he wrote. The distinguished performers of that time, Alleyn, Burbage, Heminge, Condell, Shakspeare, all appear to have died in independent, if not affluent, circumstances; but the remuneration obtained by the poet was most miserably curtailed. The price given at the theatre for a new play fluctuated between ten and twenty pounds; the copyright, if the piece was printed, might produce from six to ten pounds more; in addition to these sums, the dedication-fee may be reckoned, the usual amount of which was forty shillings. Our author appears to have produced about two or three plays every year. Most of them were successful; but, even with this industry and good fortune, his annual income would rarely have exceeded fifty pounds: and we cannot, therefore, feel surprised at finding him continually speaking of his necessities; or that the only existing document connected with his life should be one that represents him in a state of pecuniary embarrassment.

Among the papers of Dulwich College, the indefatigable Mr. Malone discovered the following letter tripartite, which, coming from persons of such deserved celebrity, cannot fail of interesting the reader.

"To our most loving friend, Mr. Phillip Hinchlow, esquire, these.

"Mr. Hinchlow,

"You understand our unfortunate extremitie, and I doe not thincke you so void of Christianitie but that you would throw so much money into the Thames as wee request now of you, rather than endanger so many innocent lives. You know there is xl. more, at least, to be receaved of you for the play. We desire you to lend us vl. of that, which shall be allowed to you; without which, we cannot be bayled, nor I play any more till this be dispatch'd. It will lose you xxl. ere the end of the next weeke, besides the hindrance of the next new play. Pray, sir, consider our cases with humanity, and now give us cause to acknowledge you our true freind in time of neede. Wee have entreated Mr. Davison to deliver this note, as well to witness your love as our promises, and always acknowledgement to be ever

"Your most thankfull and loving friends,
"NAT. FIELD."

"The money shall be abated out of the money remayns for the play of Mr. Fletcher and ours.
"ROB. DABORNE."

"I have ever found you a true loving friend to mee, and in soe small a suite, it beinge honest, I hope you will not fail us.
"PHILIP MASSINGER."

Indorsed.
"Received by mee, Robert Davison, of Mr. Hinchlow, for the use of Mr. Daboerne, Mr. Feeld, Mr. Messenger, the sum of vl.
"ROB. DAVISON."

The occasion of the distress in which these three distinguished persons were involved it is not possible to fathom. We may imagine a thousand emergencies, either creditable or discreditable to the fame of the writers, with which the letter would perfectly tally; but, on such slight and vague intimations, no ingenuity could determine which was most likely to be correct. But from the document a circumstance is ascertained, which, before its discovery, had been called in question. Sir Aston Cockayne, a friend of Massinger, had asserted in a volume of poems, published in 1658, that our author had written in conjunction with Fletcher; Davies doubted this report, but the above letter establishes the fact beyond the possibility of dispute.

Massinger is known to have produced thirty-seven plays for the stage, a list of which is given at the conclusion of this memoir. Sixteen entire plays and the fragment of another, The Parliament of Love, alone are extant. No less than eleven of his productions, in manuscript, were in possession of Mr. Warburton (Somerset Herald), and destroyed with the rest of that gentleman's invaluable collection by his cook, who, ignorant of their worth, used them as waste paper for the purposes of the kitchen.

The great and various merits of the works of Massinger will be better seen in the following volumes than in any elaborate, critical dissertation. If our author be compared with the other dramatic writers of his age, we cannot long hesitate where to place him. More natural in his characters and more poetical in his diction than Jonson or Cartwright, more elevated and nervous than Fletcher, the only writers who can be supposed to contest his pre-eminence, Massinger ranks immediately under Shakspeare himself. Our poet excels, perhaps, more in the description than in the expression of passion; this may in some measure be ascribed to his attention to the fable: while his scenes are managed with consummate skill, the lighter shades of character and sentiment are lost in the tendency of each part to the catastrophe. The melody, force, and variety of his versification are always remarkable. The prevailing beauties of his productions are dignity and elegance; their predominant fault is want of passion.

Massinger's last play—which is unfortunately lost—The Anchoress of Pausilippo, was acted Jan. 26, 1640, about six weeks before his death, which happened on the 17th of March, 1640. He went to bed in good health, says Langbaine, and was found dead in the morning, in his own house on the Bankside. He was buried in the churchyard of St. Saviour's, and the comedians paid the last sad duty to his name, by attending him to the grave.

It does not appear, though every stone and every fragment of a stone has been carefully examined, that any monument or inscription of any kind marked the place where his dust was deposited. "The memorial of his mortality," says Gifford, "is given with a pathetic brevity, which accords but too well with the obscure and humble passages of his life: March 20, 1639-40, buried Philip Massinger, A STRANGER."

Such is all the information that remains to us of this distinguished poet. But though we are ignorant of every circumstance respecting him but that he lived, wrote, and died, we may yet form some idea of his personal character from the recommendatory poems prefixed to his several plays, in which, as Mr. Gifford justly observes, the language of his panegyrists, though warm, expresses an attachment apparently derived not so much from his talents as his virtues: he is their beloved, much-esteemed, dear, worthy, deserving, honoured, long-known, and long-loved friend. All the writers of his life represent him as a man of singular modesty, gentleness, candour, and affability; nor does it appear that he ever made or found an enemy.

PHILIP MASSINGER – A CONCISE BIBLIOGRAPHY

As would be expected many works from this time no longer exist either in part or their entirety. Further many playwrights collaborated on plays or revised them for later performances and we have used the latest position known on each of them for the bibliography below.

Solo Plays
The Maid of Honour, tragicomedy (c. 1621; printed 1632)
The Duke of Milan, tragedy (c. 1621–3; printed 1623, 1638)
The Unnatural Combat, tragedy (c. 1621–6; printed 1639)
The Bondman, tragicomedy (licensed 3 December 1623; printed 1624)
The Renegado, tragicomedy (licensed 17 April 1624; printed 1630)
The Parliament of Love, comedy (licensed 3 November 1624; MS)

A New Way to Pay Old Debts, comedy (c. 1625; printed 1632)
The Roman Actor, tragedy (licensed 11 October 1626; printed 1629)
The Great Duke of Florence, tragicomedy (licensed 5 July 1627; printed 1636)
The Picture, tragicomedy (licensed 8 June 1629; printed 1630)
The Emperor of the East, tragicomedy (licensed 11 March 1631; printed 1632)
Believe as You List, tragedy (rejected by the censor in January, but licensed 6 May 1631; MS)
The City Madam, comedy (licensed 25 May 1632; printed 1658)
The Guardian, comedy (licensed 31 October 1633; printed 1655)
The Bashful Lover, tragicomedy (licensed 9 May 1636; printed 1655)

Collaborations with John Fletcher
Sir John van Olden Barnavelt, tragedy (August 1619; MS)
The Little French Lawyer, comedy (c. 1619–23; printed 1647)
A Very Woman, tragicomedy (c. 1619–22; licensed 6 June 1634; printed 1655)
The Custom of the Country, comedy (c. 1619–23; printed 1647)
The Double Marriage, tragedy (c. 1619–23; Printed 1647)
The False One, history (c. 1619–23; printed 1647)
The Prophetess, tragicomedy (licensed 14 May 1622; printed 1647)
The Sea Voyage, comedy (licensed 22 June 1622; printed 1647)
The Spanish Curate, comedy (licensed 24 October 1622; printed 1647)
The Lovers' Progress or The Wandering Lovers, tragicomedy (licensed Dec 1623; rev 1634; printed 1647)
The Elder Brother, comedy (c. 1625; printed 1637).

Collaborations with John Fletcher and Francis Beaumont
Thierry and Theodoret, tragedy (c. 1607; printed 1621)
The Coxcomb, comedy (1608–10; printed 1647)
Beggars' Bush, comedy (c. 1612–15; revised 1622; printed 1647)
Love's Cure, comedy (c. 1612–15; revised 1625; printed 1647).

Collaborations with John Fletcher and Nathan Field
The Honest Man's Fortune, tragicomedy (1613; printed 1647)
The Queen of Corinth, tragicomedy (c. 1616–18; printed 1647)
The Knight of Malta, tragicomedy (c. 1619; printed 1647).

Collaborations with Nathan Field
The Fatal Dowry, tragedy (c. 1619, printed 1632); adapted by Nicholas Rowe: The Fair Penitent

Collaborations with John Fletcher, John Ford, and William Rowley, or John Webster
The Fair Maid of the Inn, comedy (licensed 22 January 1626; printed 1647).

Collaborations with John Fletcher, Ben Jonson, and George Chapman
Rollo Duke of Normandy, or The Bloody Brother, tragedy (c. 1616–24; printed 1639).

Collaborations with Thomas Dekker
The Virgin Martyr, tragedy (licensed 6 October 1620; printed 1622).

Collaborations with Thomas Middleton and William Rowley
The Old Law, comedy (c. 1615–18; printed 1656).

www.ingramcontent.com/pod-product-compliance
Lightning Source LLC
Chambersburg PA
CBHW060122050426
42448CB00010B/1989

* 9 781787 373112 *